LIFE & DEATH:

A Buddhist Perspective

by
James Hilgendorf

Along with Panelists:

Margie Hall
Eric Hauber
Theresa Hauber
Shinji Ishibashi

Library of Congress Control Number: 2002091020

ISBN 1-929159-16-1

Excerpts from Memories, Dreams and Reflections, by C. G. Jung, edited by Aniela Jaffe, translated by Richard & Clara Winston, copyright 1961, 1962, 1963 and renewed 1989, 1990, 1991 by Random House, Inc. Used by permission of Pantheon Books, a division of Random House, Inc.

Excerpts from The Tao of Physics, by Fritjof Capra, 25th anniversary edition, 2000, reprinted by arrangement with Shambhala Publications, Inc., Boston, www.shambhala.com.

Excerpts from There is a River, by Thomas Sugrue, revised edition, May, 1989, reprinted by permission of the Edgar Cayce Foundation, Virginia Beach, VA.

Excerpts from the following works of Daisaku Ikeda: The Living Buddha; The Human Revolution; Unlocking the Mysteries of Birth and Death, Buddhism in the Contemporary World; Life: An Enigma, A Precious Jewel; Human Values in a Changing World; and quotes from The Writings of Nichiren Daishonin, Soka Gakkai, 1999, reprinted with permission of the Soka Gakkai, Tokyo, Japan.

Published by The Tribute Series, P. O. Box 195, Vida, OR. 97488
(800) 898-9441.

CONTENTS

ACKNOWLEDGMENTS

Thanks to the following people for their participation, encouragement, and help in putting together this book.

For the panelists on the Life & Death: A Buddhist Perspective panel discussion: Margie Hall, Eric Hauber, Theresa Hauber, and Shinji Ishibashi, and to the following who helped stage the panel discussion: Eileen McGruder, Susan Hirahara, Steve Davis, Lavelle Roby, Mark Justin, Leon Jones, Jessie Goins and Alan Ruskin; to Ling Ling Chen, for her extraordinary experience; to Raymond Foti, a great friend; to Lee Arnone, for his encouragement; to my wife Elizabeth Hilgendorf, with my deepest love, for her extraordinary and incomparable support over the years; to the following people who were the initiators of the weekly discussions that led to this book: Pontip Thammaruja, Diane Lopez, and Harold Jeffries. In the spirit of the discussion herein,this book is dedicated to the eternal memory of Roy and Dorothy Hilgendorf, and Bert, Ruth, and Gretchen Housman, without whose love and support this book would never have been written. And to Daisaku Ikeda, for his vision, courage and unparalleled efforts towards world peace, culture, education, and the happiness of humanity.

James Hilgendorf

LIFE & DEATH:

A Buddhist Perspective

INTRODUCTION

In the 13th century, Nichiren Daishonin, a great revolutionary Buddhist sage, wrote:

> "If you truly want to understand life, you must first study death."

Death is the most democratic of experiences. All of us inevitably meet our end at some point in time. But in our high-tech, western culture, death is somehow the last thing we like to talk or think about. For many people, only when facing their imminent demise, through disease or old age or war or whatever, do they face the disturbing final questions.

But as Nichiren Daishonin was intimating, only when we come to grips with death, can we fully live. For death, and our understanding of it, gives meaning - or the lack of meaning - to our lives.

In Tolstoy's great novella, "The Death of Ivan Ilyich," this point is driven home in an extraordinarily poignant fashion. The story follows an official in the Russian government, Ivan Ilyich, who leads a rather normal life, with family and career and the struggles of everyday life occupying his time and thoughts, until suddenly, in his mid-forties, he comes down with a strange and progressively fatal disease. At first, he is only a little worried. Then, as the pain increases, he is forced to confront the possibility of his death. The reality of his own approaching death becomes unbearable and overwhelming. He is forced to search for answers, to struggle with his own mortality, to re-evaluate all that he has been or done. It is only during the last moments of his life, on his death-bed, that he finds some answers; and in those moments, his life is utterly transformed.

But more of that later....

Life and death are all around us, as common as water and the air we breath. Every moment, life is coming into being, plants and animals, men and women, distant stars and suns and moons, in dazzling variety; and each moment an equal infinity of beings and galaxies expire and take their exit from the stage of life.

What is the meaning of it all? Is there any meaning? What is life? What is death?

These are questions we will address in this book.

As the title of this book indicates, a Buddhist perspective underlies this book; but we will be exploring the question of life and death from many different perspectives - from the perspective of science, of physics, of relativity theory, quantum mechanics, string theory, holographic theory and evolution; from the perspective of other religions; of philosophy and psychology, the work of Carl Jung, and Edgar Cayce, and adding in the voluminous research done on near-death experiences, including the work of Elisabeth Kubler-Ross, Raymood Moody, Dr. Kenneth Ring and others.

The purpose in touching upon these many different disciplines and approaches is to pose questions, stimulate curiosity, and open further paths of inquiry.

For a basic tenet of this book is that, if there is a single underlying truth and reality about our universe, then religion, science, psychology, and even simple common sense should all help to illuminate that reality. All of them should point in a common direction, and help us understand how we fit in with the cosmos around us. We may never be able to comprehend the grand scheme of things, and, at its heart, the universe may forever remain inscrutable; but I have no doubt that we can begin to decipher our own relations to the workings of the universe, to life and death, and this is, after all, of utmost importance to the way we live our lives, and to our happiness.

I am no expert on the subject of life and death. I am not a scholar, nor am I an expert on religion or science or psychology. I stress this, because during the entire book, I will be taking the approach of a layman, or an ordinary person, looking for answers. I am still looking for answers. I believe, after all, that the subject of death is something you have to subjectively come to grips with by yourself. What seems obvious or sensible to me may not seem so to you, and vice versa. But I do believe that if each of us searches long and hard enough, we will uncover answers, or at least the intimations of answers. I also believe that in the process of searching for answers, your life and understanding will deepen immeasurably, and that you will become a richer person, even though you may not actually find complete answers.

There are many different forms of Buddhism, just as there are many kinds of Christianity. In this book, we will touch briefly on the historical development of Buddhism; but much of the material will reflect the views of a particular type of Buddhism, that of the SGI, or Soka Gakkai International. This Buddhism originated with Nichiren Daishonin in the thirteenth century, and is based on the chanting of the words Nam Myoho Renge Kyo. But it is also directly linked to the teachings of the historical

Buddha, Shakyamuni, and especially to the teachings he expounded during the last eight years of his life, the Lotus Sutra. The SGI is an international lay organization, with, to date, over twelve million members practicing in 187 countries around the world.

In Buddhism, there is no conflict between religion and science. Buddhism accepts the findings of science, and uses them to help clarify the workings of the universe around us.

Does life continue after death? If so, in what way? What is the relation of life to death? These are the answers we seek; and all of the approaches we will touch on can help to shed light on these questions. I would simply add, from my own experience, that Nichiren Daishonin's Buddhism provides the clearest, most comprehensive, picture of the whole that I have thus far encountered.

In the second part of this book, I have presented a transcript of a panel discussion that took place in July, 2000, in Los Angeles. The panelists were all members of the SGI. The discussion, and the subsequent question and answer session with the audience, provide many practical and profound insights and experiences surrounding this whole question of life and death.

The book concludes with a woman's experience.

May this book give understanding and hope to all its readers.

chapter

1

A SHORT HISTORY OF BUDDHISM

First of all, I would like to present some background about Buddhism.

There are many different forms of Buddhism; but they all stem out of the life and teachings of one person, Shakyamuni, or Gautama Buddha. The exact dates of his birth and death are not exactly known, but a good estimate is that he lived somewhere around the sixth century B.C.

He was born as prince Siddhartha, the son of a king named Shuddhodana, and his wife, queen Maya. The young prince was brought up in great luxury, protected from the outside world. Shakyamuni himself later recalled his upbringing:

> "I was delicately nurtured, exceedingly delicately nurtured, delicately nurtured beyond measure. In my father's residence, lotus-ponds were made; one of blue lotuses, one of red and another of white lotuses, just for my sake....I had three palaces, one for winter, one for summer and one for the rainy season...in the rainy season palace, during the four

> months of the rains, entertained only by female musicians, I did not come down from the palace."

The turning point in his life came when he was 29 years old. On several occasions, while out driving with his charioteer, Siddhartha encountered old, sick, and dying people, and he was deeply troubled by these experiences. On another occasion, he came upon a wandering ascetic, wearing a yellow robe. Siddhartha was deeply impressed with the man's peaceful demeanor, in the midst of so much misery. On returning to his palace, Siddhartha decided to renounce his princely life and become a wanderer, searching for the Truth and for an answer to the sufferings that plagued all people, those of birth, old age, sickness, and death.

For several years, he practiced severe austerities and extreme self-mortification. He later described himself thus:

> "Because of so little nourishment, all my limbs became like some withered creepers with knotted joints; my backbone protruding like a string of balls; my ribs like rafters of a dilapidated shed; the pupils of my eyes appeared sunk deep in their sockets as water appears shining at the bottom of a deep well."

From these experiences, however, he finally realized that such austerities could not lead him to the Truth he sought. He therefore changed his way of life, and once again began to eat proper amounts of food.

When he was 35, he sat down one evening beneath a bodhi tree, determined not to rise up until he had attained Enlightenment.

During the first part of the night, he waged a fierce struggle with demons within himself. Having vanquished them, he spent the rest of the night in deep meditation, finally attaining his own enlightenment.

What was the nature of this enlightenment? Daisaku Ikeda, third president of the SGI, gives his own assessment:

> "When we look dispassionately at the great universe around us, we find that what at first glance appears to be a vast stillness is in fact constantly throbbing with creation and change. The same is true of man; he ages, dies, is reborn, and dies again. Nothing, either in the world of nature or that of human society, knows a moment of stagnation or rest. All things in the universe are in flux, arising and ceasing, appearing and disappearing, caught in an unending cycle of change that is conditioned by the law of causation at work both temporally and spacially. Such is the nature of ultimate reality. My conviction is that Shakyamuni's enlightenment was in a sense a cry of wonder at the mysterious entity called life, whose manifestations are joined to and dependent upon one another through the links of cause and effect. But ordinary people are unaware of this truth and delude themselves into believing that they exist independently of one another. Such a delusion estranges them from the Law of Life, which is the ultimate truth, and causes them to become the prisoners of desire."

During the next several weeks, Shakyamuni spent time meditating on the various aspects of his experience. Then he commenced his journey, which he would continue until his death at age 80, to share with people the Truth he had realized.

His first sermon was given in a deer park in Sarnath, near Varanasi, in India. In this sermon, often called the sermon of the Middle Way, he expounded the Four Noble Truths - that change and suffering is universal; that suffering is caused by desire; that suffering can be overcome; and that there is a Way leading to freedom from suffering, which is the Middle Way of right conduct, right motive, right resolve, right speech, right livelihood, right attention, right effort and right meditation.

Another tenet of his teachings was ahimsa, or non-violence. He also refused to recognize the caste system that was a long-established institution in India. He believed in the absolute equality of people. He was concerned with developing the potential within all human beings.

During his lifetime, Shakyamuni traveled over much of India on foot, preaching and raising disciples. He was an extraordinary teacher. He had the ability to adapt his teachings to the capacity of his hearers, no matter who they were. It was said that even those who came to challenge Shakyamuni in debate became his disciples in the end.

He was a man of wisdom and great compassion, who was moved by the spectacle of human suffering and was determined to teach his fellow human beings how that suffering could be confronted and overcome.

Many of his teachings were what we might call "expedient" teachings. The truth to which Shakyamuni had become enlightened was exceedingly difficult to relay to other people; so he chose different means, depending upon each individual's situation, to convey something of that truth.

In one case, for instance, he encountered a grieving woman who had lost her child. The woman wanted to know why her child had died. Shakyamuni said he would tell her the answer; but only on the condition that she first find someone in the city who had never been afflicted with the death of a loved one. The woman went door to door, talking to people; but everywhere she went, she found men and women who had suffered the loss of a loved one. There was no one who was untouched by death. Little by little, the woman realized that in her suffering she was not alone. She began to feel more deeply the sufferings of others. Her life expanded. She sought answers to the deep questions of life. This was Shakyamuni's deep compassion in action.

His teachings are said to have filled eighty-four thousand volumes. Just as with the woman suffering from the loss of a loved one, Shakyamuni employed many different "expedient means" to remove peoples' suffering and to lead them to the Truth. Many sects of Buddhism, however, later developed from these partial or incomplete teachings, and enshrined these partial truths as The Truth.

For instance,Shakyamuni at first put great emphasis upon discarding attachments to the mundane world, and to such goals as wealth, fame and power; not because in and of themselves they were wrong; but rather that, as part of a constantly changing world, they cannot bring lasting happiness, and distract us from the true purpose of life. By first denouncing attachments, Shakyamuni sought to awaken his hearers to the shallowness of their own views of life.

Shakyamuni taught that change and suffering are inherent in life. For many, this developed into a feeling that Buddhism is basically pessimistic; that its fundamental message is that life is filled with suffering, and that the goal of Buddhist practice is to somehow to escape from life, to cut ourselves off from our desires, and achieve a release from suffering and from life itself. This is not so. There is no escaping from desires. Rather, our desires are themselves the fuel for achieving our enlightenment.

These "expedient" teachings - which represented only partial aspects of the Truth - were many times erroneously perceived as the totality of what Shakyamuni was trying to convey. As a result, different sects of Buddhism, embodying these partial teachings, came into existence.

It was only in the last eight years of his life that Shakyamuni began to preach directly from his own enlightenment. These teachings became known as the Lotus Sutra. The Lotus Sutra is an extraordinary, fantastic work of literature, which was only written down in its present form long after Shakyamuni lived; but the core of the Lotus Sutra still resonates with his words and heart and eternal enlightenment.

In the Lotus Sutra, Shakyamuni suddenly announces to the multitude gathered around him that up until now, although he had expounded many doctrines, he had not yet revealed the Truth.

A great Treasure Tower, half as large as the earth itself and adorned with precious jewels appears and rises into the air. An almost infinite number of Buddhas and other great beings, shining in the enlightened aspect of their lives, converge on this Treasure Tower from universes beyond imagining, beyond time and space, to lend credence to the truth which Shakyamuni is about to expound.

Shakyamuni reveals that, contrary to what everyone believes, that he first attained enlightenment in his present lifetime while meditating under a bodhi tree; he had, in fact, actually become enlightened in the unimaginably remote past, millions and millions of eons ago, and had ever since then been in this world preaching the Law. The life of the Buddha is eternal. He predicts that each of his followers, and even his greatest enemies, will, in the future, become Buddhas too.

The significance of the Lotus Sutra is this: The Treasure Tower, in all its splendor and magnificence, represents the great enlightened state of life of the Buddha, overflowing with life force, wisdom and compassion. But it is also, without exception, our own life as well. We are all Buddhas, unawakened to this fact. Our lives are eternal. The Buddha's mission was to awaken all people to this truth.

After his death, his teachings fragmented into many different sects of Buddhism. Shakyamuni was elevated to the status of a god. But this had never been his intent. He was no god. He was a simple human being, and the simple human being is the Buddha. This was his message, and the message of the Lotus Sutra.

Shakyamuni' s teachings were voluminous, and in ensuing centuries there arose great confusion and debate about which of his teachings actually embodied his highest and truest intent.

In thirteenth century Japan, a young man spent almost twenty years studying the different sects and sutras of Buddhism, and resurrected to its true place, as it were, this highest teaching of Buddhism, the Lotus Sutra. In 1253 he began expounding the chanting of the words Nam Myoho Renge Kyo, the title of the sutra, as a way of bringing forth the enlightened state of life inherent within each individual. His name was Nichiren Daishonin.

He drew forth enormous opposition from the Shogunate government and from the other official reigning sects of Buddhism at the time, to the point where he was exiled twice and nearly beheaded. But Nichiren was unyielding. At the core of his beliefs was the conviction that all of the enormous troubles that were then besetting Japan and its people were the direct result of one single thing - the fact that the people had all abandoned the Lotus Sutra and its teachings, and were now giving their allegiance to inferior religions which fostered an incorrect view of life.

Why was the Lotus Sutra so special? Because it was the only teaching of Shakyamuni's in which he revealed the eternity of life and the absolute equality of the Buddha nature within all living beings. To practice any other lesser forms of Buddhism, in essence, was to deny the splendor and magnificent potential for Buddhahood and absolute happiness existing within each and every human being. In one of his letters, Nichiren wrote:

> "In Buddhism, that teaching is judged supreme which enables everyone, whether good or evil, to become Buddhas."

The reciting of the Lotus Sutra and the chanting of Nam Myoho Renge Kyo was the means of uniting the microcosm of the human being with the macrocosm of the great universe, and causing the power and rhythm of the universe itself to begin to function within the individual's life, bringing great benefit, joy, and the power to surmount and overcome any suffering and difficulty whatsoever in life.

Nichiren died in 1282, leaving behind many writings. His disciples carried on his teachings for the next several hundred years; but it was not until the 1930's that the time for the full-scale dissemination of his teachings seemed at last to have arrived.

In 1930, a Japanese educator, Tsunesaburo Makiguchi, converted to the teachings of Nichiren. His closest assistant, Josei Toda, followed suit. Together they founded a lay organization, the precursor of the present-day SGI, or Soka Gakkai International. The lay organization began to slowly grow. By the outbreak of World War II, its membership counted about three thousand families.

As the war progressed, however, increasing pressure was brought to bear by the government to suppress religious organizations that did not show strict obeisance to the emperor, the militaristic government, and to the official State religion, Shinto. Makiguchi resolutely stood up against this pressure. He absolutely opposed militarism and the war. He refused to submit to the Shinto hierarchy, which was in league with the government.

As a result, Makiguchi was imprisoned, along with his disciple, Josei Toda, and other Soka Gakkai members. After interrogation and torture, only Makiguchi and Toda still refused to give up their faith and remained in prison. At the end of two years of imprisonment, Makiguchi, the first president of the Soka Gakkai, died in prison.

Torn with grief, Toda remained on alone. In his cold prison cell, he pondered the Lotus Sutra over and over, while chanting Nam Myoho Renge Kyo ten thousand times a day.

One day, in March, 1944, he was re-reading some lines from the Lotus Sutra that kept puzzling him. They were a description of the entity of the Buddha, expressed in thirty-four negations:

> "His body neither existing nor not existing,
> neither caused nor conditioned, neither self nor other,
> neither square nor round, neither short nor long,

neither appearing nor disappearing,
neither born nor extinguished,
neither created nor arising, neither acted nor made,
neither sitting nor lying down,
neither walking nor standing,
neither moving nor turning, neither idle nor still,
neither advancing nor retreating,
neither in safety nor in danger,
neither right nor wrong, neither gaining nor losing,
neither that nor this, neither departing nor coming,
neither blue nor yellow, neither red nor white,
neither crimson nor purple nor any other sort of color."

Over and over, Toda tried with his whole life to understand these lines. He later recounted his experience in the third person in an autobiographical novel titled The Human Revolution.

> "As Mr. Gan read the 'Virtuous Practices' chapter of the Sutra of Immeasurable Meanings and reached the verse containing the thirty-four negations, there, in the deep recesses of the thick spectacles he wore, a brilliant white light flashed in his eyes. It was no longer his eyes that were moving down the page. Neither was he reading the sutra with his intellect: He was pounding his still robust body against each word and phrase of the verse."

Suddenly the word 'life' flashed through his mind. And in that instant, by substituting the word 'life' for entity, he arrived at a complete awareness of the meaning of the lines.

"*Life* is neither existing nor not existing,
neither caused nor conditioned, neither self nor other,
neither square nor round, neither short nor long,
neither crimson nor purple nor any other sort of color."

The Buddha is life itself. It exists within ourselves, and outside our lives as well. It is the life of the entire universe. Everyone and everything inherently possesses Buddhahood. And the way to tap and bring out the immense state of Buddhahood from within our lives is through the chanting of Nam Myoho Renge Kyo.

Shortly thereafter, Toda, his health shattered, was released from prison. Japan lay in ruins. The Soka Gakkai organization lay in ruins.

But deep within Toda's heart there now burned an unquenchable sense of mission. His dream, like his mentor's before him, was nothing less than erasing unhappiness from the lives of people the world over.

He began holding small discussion meetings, lecturing on the Lotus Sutra, Nichiren Daishonin's teachings, and Nam Myoho Renge Kyo. Like Shakyamuni, he focused on relieving the sufferings of ordinary people.

In 1948, a young man, upon hearing Toda speak one evening, joined the Soka Gakkai. He gradually became Toda's closest disciple and eventual successor. His name was Daisaku Ikeda.

When Josei Toda died in 1957, the membership of the Soka Gakkai had grown to an astonishing 750,000 households. Under Mr. Ikeda, at the beginning of the twenty-first century the Soka Gakkai has grown to 12,000,000 members in 180 countries throughout the world.

A few years after his release from prison, Josei Toda began putting down on paper some of his thoughts about life and death. In The Philosophy of Life, he wrote:

"Living a lonesome life in a cold prison cell because of an unfounded accusation, I plunged myself deeply into thought and introspection, and eventually probed the complex issue of the 'substance of human life,' which I believe to be the essential point facing us.

"What is human life? Does it exist only in this world? Does it last for eternity? These are eternal riddles for all mankind. From ancient days, those respected as great sages or distinguished persons desperately sought answers to these questions, each in his own way."

He continued, trying to use simple examples that would be readily understandable by anyone.

"A person may feel delight, but with time, this feeling passes...It does not necessarily go away, but you cannot relocate it since it melts back into the mind itself.

Several hours or several days later, however, the same feeling of delight may arise. In another example, suppose someone is grief-stricken over something. Several hours or days later, as he recalls the happening, the same grief may envelop him. People may say that he renews his sad feelings by himself, but there is certainly a continuation of the earlier and later griefs, while at the same time there is no visible link between them.

"Similar phenomena occur when we sleep each night. The mind, or consciousness, does not 'exist' while a person is asleep, but the moment he awakens, his mind begins its activities again. Thus, we can say that there is no mind while one is sleeping, but there is a mind while one is awake. Which is true - to say that there is a mind or that there is not a mind? If we choose to say that it exists, we cannot always find it. In contrast, if we choose to say that it does not exist, suddenly it appears.

"The universe itself is life. Suppose we die. After death, life is fused into the great life of the universe and can be found nowhere, just as there is no connection between moments of grief or between moments of delight, or as there is no mind while one is asleep. For a thing called a 'soul' to be navigating the heavens is not a valid theory. Even if life melts into the great universe, it does not always feel repose, just as sleep is not necessarily restful. While we sleep, some find peace; others are tortured by bad dreams, and others worry about their light slumber.

"Thus, just as one sleeps and awakens, and awakens and sleeps, man lives and dies, and dies and lives, maintaining the eternity of life."

chapter

2

"ESHO FUNI"

In 1543, Nicolaus Copernicus published his work "On The Revolutions of the Celestial Spheres." For a thousand years or more, the old Ptolemaic system of looking at the universe had held sway, namely a system that pictured the universe as geocentric, or revolving around the Earth, with Man at its center. Now Copernicus was proposing a model of the solar system which centered on the Sun.

In the century that followed, others began probing the nature of the universe about them. Tycho Brahe painstakingly collected data about the motions of heavenly bodies. He passed this data on to his pupil, Johannes Kepler, who, in turn, developed the laws of motion which became the groundwork for Sir Isaac Newton's monumental work, Mathematical Principles of Natural Philosophy, which revolutionized our understanding of the natural world.

Galileo Galilei helped develop the astronomical telescope, discovering craters on the Moon, sunspots, and the satellites of Jupiter. He showed the Milky Way is composed of stars.

Galileo's astronomical observations led him to uphold the Copernican theory that the planets revolve around the Sun. This conflicted with the teachings of the Roman Catholic Church, however, and Galileo was forced to recant his findings and was placed under house arrest for the final eight years of his life.

What was evolving through this century was a world view very much at odds with the religious cosmology of the Catholic Church that had held sway for a thousand years. Even though many argued that these new discoveries actually confirmed the views of Christianity, and proved the greatness and glory of God, an undeniable shift had taken place in men and women's minds.

It was a new rationalism that was emerging, and at the heart of this battle of ideas, perhaps there was no more prime architect than the Frenchman Rene Descartes. His was a crucial figure in the history of philosophy, and the influence of his ideas still permeates and shapes western thought and civilization today.

Descartes was deeply influenced by Galileo. He was also a great mathematician, who invented analytic geometry.

In his treatise, Discourse on Method, published in 1637, Descartes sought to tear down old structures of thought and to establish the most fundamental truths upon which to build up his philosophy. His searches brought him to the bedrock certainty of self-consciousness. "Cogito; ergo sum." I think, therefore I am. This was his famous declaration. This became his unshakable starting point.

Inherent in Descartes' philosophy, was a complete split between mind and matter. On the one hand was the spiritual self, and on the other hand there was the mechanistic world outside the self. There was always this dualism of mind as a spiritual principal, and matter as mere spatial extension. The self, or mind, was alive and spiritual, but beyond the self lay the insensate world of matter.

Descartes' ideas permeated the century and had profound implications and consequences. Sir Isaac Newton's scientific work was a perfect reflection of these ideas.

Newton's universe was a mechanistic universe, governed by strict laws of mathematics. Arising out of his work, and others, there grew up the belief that man could ultimately fathom and master the mechanics of the universe itself and harness its powers to work for his benefit. Implicit in this new science was the idea of an objective, static universe that was external to man and did not depend upon outside forces for its functioning. Newton himself and Descartes argued for the existence of God in the greater scheme of things; but it was a mere step to ask: Why God? The universe and its laws existed, and man existed; but was God necessary? As an acknowledgment of the threat posed by Descartes' ideas, the Catholic Church banned his books.

This way of looking at things has profoundly shaped our lives even today. In Western civilization, we are unconsciously raised to view the world about us in a certain way. This way of looking at things is as natural as breathing, or the water that a fish swims about in. It is taken utterly for granted.

We are not a part of nature. We are not a part of the environment around us. Of course, we know we live in an environment, and we know we are part of it in that sense. But at the deepest level, there is always a distinction between ourselves, the living individual, and the world around us. There is always a fundamental split, a distinction. We are different. We are individuals, we possess a mind, a spirit, a soul; and everything around us is different, it is soulless or inanimate. Descartes himself actually argued that animals were automatons, that they were part of the mechanistic world that surrounds us.

This dualistic view of life has profound consequences. It means we can act upon the world around us as we see fit. It means we can manipulate the environment around us to our own advantage, without any apparent consequences to our own lives. It means that we are the lords of creation, and everything beyond the human being is subservient, soulless, and subject to our control.

Our Judeo-Christian heritage reinforces this basic world-view. In Genesis, in the Bible, it reads that in the beginning:

> "God created humankind
> in his image,
> in the image of God he
> created them;
> male and female he
> created them.
>
> "God blessed them, and God said to them, 'Be fruitful and multiply, and fill the earth and subdue it; and have dominion over the fish of the sea and over the birds of the air and over every living thing that moves upon the earth."

Our immediate predecessors in this land called America had a completely different way of looking at things. The American Indian was a part of nature, not separate from it. The Indian was not the sole lord of creation, but only one of many inhabitants of a diverse universe.

John Muir, the great American naturalist, writer and conservationist, who spent years in Yosemite and the Sierras, once wrote of the Indian's and the white man's different impacts upon the California environment:

"How many centuries Indians have roamed these woods nobody knows, probably a great many, extending far beyond the time that Columbus touched our shores, and it seems strange that heavier marks have not been made. Indians walk softly and hurt the landscape hardly more than the birds and squirrels, and their brush and bark huts last hardly longer than those of wood rats, while their more enduring monuments, excepting those wrought on the forests by the fires they made to improve their hunting grounds, vanish in a few centuries.

"How different are most of those of the white man, especially on the lower gold region - roads blasted in the solid rock, wild streams dammed and tamed and turned out of their channels and led along the sides of canyons and valleys to work in mines like slaves. Crossing from ridge to ridge, high in the air, on long straddling trestles as if flowing on stilts, or down and up across valleys and hills imprisoned in iron pipes to strike and wash away hills and the skin of the mountain's face, riddling, stripping every gold gully and flat. These are the white man's marks made in a few feverish years, to say nothing of mills, fields, villages, scattered hundreds of miles along the flank of the range. Long will it be ere these marks are effaced, though Nature does what she can, replanting, gardening, sweeping away old dams and flumes, leveling gravel and boulder piles, patiently trying to heal every raw scar."

This process of indiscriminate use has only accelerated since then. At the heart of most of our endeavor is the profit motive. Use anything, destroy anything, decimate anything, as long as it yields a profit. This type of thinking has come to dominate and penetrate almost the entire earth. At the core of this type of behavior is the belief we are the god-given arbiters and rulers of the earth. There is something in our mentality in western society that disregards the environment about us. We can only see the environment as something to use, to manipulate, to torture into our service.

Where has this type of thinking and action led us? To the brink of ecological disaster. Poisoning of the rivers and oceans of the world. Poisoning and depletion of the land. Cancer. Wholesale destruction of fish and wildlife. Incredible air pollution, noise pollution, spiritual confusion. Destruction of the community and family. And the list goes on.

Something is wrong, but what?

Buddhism has a way of looking at this problem, which can be summed up in the term "Esho Funi". "Esho" is the combination of the first syllables of two words - "eho", the object or environment, and "shoho", the living subject. Shoho are living beings and eho their environment. "Funi" means essentially two, but not two; identical in the depths of being.

In more concrete terms "esho funi" means the inseparability of oneself and the environment. The self and the environment are two, but not two. At the core, they are actually one.

This is difficult for the western mind to grasp. We are so used to grasping the world about us in the same way that Descartes envisioned it. It is us, and then the environment, separate things. It is the self, and then the non-self, in an adversarial position. It is mind, and matter. They are forever separate.

Buddhism views things from a profoundly different perspective. The self and its environment are inseparable. In other words, as incredible as it may seem, your actual self does not end with your body and skin, but is actually connected in a very real and profound way with everything that extends away from your body, even to the farthest reaches of the universe. To actualize Buddhahood means that both physically and spiritually your life extends to the infinity of the universe.

Nichiren Daishonin, in one of his letters, states it this way:

> "Ultimately, all phenomena are contained within one's life, down to the last particle of dust. The nine mountains and the eight seas are encompassed in one's body, and the sun, moon, and myriad stars are found in one's life. We, however, are like a blind person who is incapable of seeing the images reflected in a mirror."

From the western Judeo-Christian perspective, environmental devastation does not really affect us. Oh, we may observe it, we may catalog it, we may think and worry about it and even take steps to rectify what is happening; but the bottom line is that in our thinking, it really has no relation to us. It is something outside ourselves. We have utterly no idea, for the most part, that the way in which we treat the environment, the animals, the rivers and streams and lakes and oceans and air and trees, has any relation, except an external relation, to our lives at all.

The reality, however, from a Buddhist perspective, is that everything we are doing to the environment, we are actually, and in the deepest, most real sense, doing to ourselves. Every oil spill that desecrates our waters and coastlines is not an isolated event that we can contain and ignore. We have desecrated a part of our own collective body and soul and psyche. The damage has already taken place. We may not see it immediately, but we will ultimately feel and experience it in the deepest part of our lives in the form of disease and rising stress and violence.

A great deal of criticism has been directed at certain pieces of environmental legislation, such as protection for the spotted owl and other species. The protection sometimes seems overblown in proportion to the apparent insignificance of a certain species in the overall scheme of things. But viewed from the health of the biosphere, of the interconnectedness of all life, the disappearance of any species is like a harbinger of what's coming, it is a warning about the future. Not only the future of that species, but about *our future*. The disappearance of any species from our environment perfectly reflects the fact that some living, breathing dimension of our own inner life is also disappearing. And it does not simply apply to someone else, it applies to each and every one of us, without exception. This is the truth of the way Buddhism sees things.

The concept of esho funi makes us ponder our relationship to our environment very carefully. Everything that is happening around us mirrors what is going on inside. A disease like aids seems to come from out of nowhere, spreading with devastating force. We desperately search for the cause and a way to stem the tide of this disease. But its spread continues unabated. What is happening within our own bodies is perfectly mirroring what is happening to the environment - the pollution, the poisoning of the rivers and lakes and oceans. Our collective bloodstream, the ocean of humanity's bloodstream, is being poisoned. And it affects us all. We may think it is happening to someone else, or in some other part of the world, but there is no escaping the spread of the disease, its penetration into our immediate surrounding personal world. We are all connected. This connectedness is what Buddhism calls dependent origination. In the depths of life, everything in the universe is constantly changing, and yet every single thing is connected to and dependent upon everything else.

Nichiren Daishonin, in a letter written to a disciple in 1275, spoke of this relationship of the self and the environment:

> "The ten directions are the 'environment' and living beings are 'life'. To illustrate, environment is like the shadow, and life, the body. Without the body, no shadow can exist, and without life, no environment. In the same way, life is shaped by the environment. The eyes are formed by the eastern quarter. From this we know that the tongue is formed by the southern quarter; the nose, the western; the ears, the northern; the body, all four quarters; and the mind, the center. Therefore, when the people's five sense organs break down, the four quarters and the center will be startled and shaken, and, as signs of the consequent destruction of the land, mountains will collapse, grasses and trees will wither, and rivers will run dry. When the people's eyes, ears, and other sense organs are startled and disturbed, changes will occur in the heavens, and when their minds are agitated, the earth will quake."

What he was saying, in poetic form, was that there is an integral relationship between the minds and life conditions of the people and the condition of the land or environment about them. This applies both collectively in a broad sense to the nation, as well as to the life of an individual.

The concept of esho funi has enormous personal consequences. Since everything around you is actually a perfect reflection of your life - indeed, is your life - the secret to changing your environment, whatever kind of problem that might pose, is to change *yourself*. This can only be done from within. This is what Buddhism calls the human revolution. In the past, we have had countless social revolutions and economic revolutions and political revolutions; but none of these have changed the fundamental problems of human existence. One political revolution leads to victory over the oppressor, and then the opposition becomes in its turn the oppressor, the tyrant, etc.

This has happened countless numbers of times throughout history. And yet, are we any happier? Are the basic human problems any different than those of people thousands of years ago? Meanwhile we hurtle towards destruction. It is as though we are constantly battling with shadows. We are never aware of the true source of the problem. Buddhism is utterly strict on this point. *We* are the problem. The problem is with ourselves.

This means *we* have to change. And once we change, once we affect that change from within, the world around us *has* to change. The environment then has no choice. Because you and your environment are inseparable, once you change, there is no way things around you can stay the same.

This kind of thinking deeply empowers the individual. There is no situation that is dead-end or hopeless. Because we have the power to change ourselves from within, we can overcome any problems and create happiness in our lives. Life is always changing. The key is to effect change in a positive way. The power to do this is the fundamental power of Life itself - Nam Myoho Renge Kyo.

Later on, we will explore these ideas more deeply; but for now let's turn our inquiries to science, and how science itself during this past century has radically altered its own view of the structure of reality to conform, more and more, to the views held by eastern thought and Buddhism.

chapter

3

"ESHO FUNI", "DEPENDENT ORIGINATION", AND SCIENCE

The classical physics of Sir Isaac Newton was founded upon certain basic assumptions, one of which was the notion of absolute space.

Newton stated:

> "Absolute Space, in its own nature, without regard to anything external, remains always similar and immoveable."

In other words, classical physics conceived of space as static and three-dimensional, obeying the strict laws of Euclidean geometry. This space was independent from anything existing within it.

The philosophical underpinnings of this physics was, once again, the fundamental division between the self and the world external to the self, implicit in the philosophy of Descartes. As a consequence of this way of looking at things, it was believed that the world and the universe itself could be described objectively. Scientists believed that the basic underlying laws of nature were all discoverable by man's reason; and once all these laws were uncovered, man would have complete control over nature. This objective description of nature became the ideal of all science.

But even from the beginning, there appeared faint cracks in the edifice. Certain phenomena did not conform exactly to formulas and rules. But the physics itself was so successful that these inconsistencies were generally overlooked.

The first part of the twentieth century, however, brought forth new discoveries and theories that would totally undermine the pinions of classical physics, revealing a vastly more intriguing and mysterious universe than anyone had heretofore imagined.

In the early part of the twentieth century, quantum theory and quantum mechanics came into being. Without going deeply into complex theory and mathematics, what does quantum theory in general tell us about the universe around us and of our relationship with that universe? To answer, let's look at a simple problem posed in physics that forced scientists to completely change the way they view the universe.

In classical mechanics, the problem of the motion of any particular body can be solved very precisely. If the position and velocity of a body are exactly known, then we can make predictions about its motion. For example, if we know exactly where an object is at a given moment, and we also know the velocity of the object, say ten miles per hour, we can make predictions about where the object will be at in the future. We normally assume that all of these variables can be measured very accurately for any moving body.

However, when it comes to sub-atomic particles, like electrons, these notions simply do not hold. There is no way we can simultaneously measure the position and velocity of electrons.

Let's state this again, just to be clear: *There is no way we can simultaneously measure the position and velocity of electrons.*

Well, you might ask, why can't we? Is it because we do not have measuring devices small enough or accurate enough to measure these things?

No, it is much more than that. It is that *simultaneous exact values simply do not exist*.

To our normal way of thinking, this seems very strange. An electron, our mind tells us, must be in some definite place; and if it moves, it must move with a certain velocity.

But, strangely, when scientists try to calculate these two variables at the same time, something goes wrong. They can definitely measure an electron's position; or they can measure an electron's velocity. But when they try to determine both *simultaneously*, it becomes impossible. They get all kinds of weird results.

This is really not as strange as it sounds. For example, look at the drawing below. What do you see?

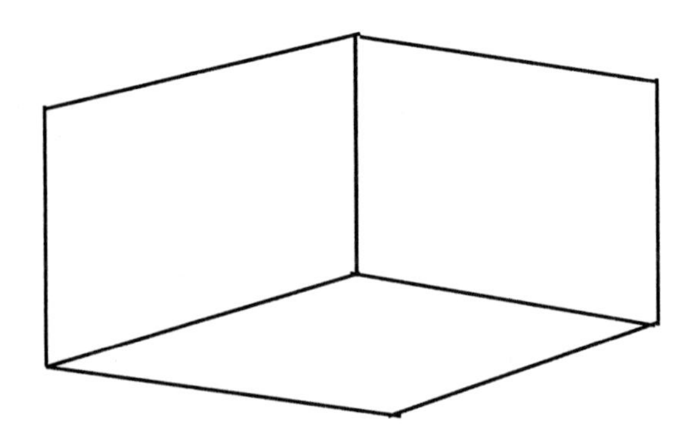

If you look at the drawing one way, you see the outside of a solid rectangular shaped structure. Look again, and suddenly you are viewing the inside of a box with only two sides standing.

Now try looking at the drawing in both of those ways at the same time.

That's right - it's impossible. We have to make a *choice*.

There is something about the processing of information of our own mind that precludes us from observing what is really there in front of our eyes except in an either/or mode. But what is really there is something different from either one. We can measure it, but only in certain ways.

In the same way, our minds naturally conceive of electrons as having a simultaneous position and velocity; but quantum theory tells us that this simply is not true. Position and velocity are two ways of looking at reality, but reality itself is something different from what we are used to perceiving.

To tackle this problem, quantum mechanics developed an entirely new approach. Simply put, instead of trying to precisely pinpoint the whereabouts and movements of particles, quantum mechanics developed, through mathematics, a way to talk about the *probability* of distribution, in space and time, of particles. By so doing, quantum mechanics became extraordinarily successful, opening up vast new vistas and practical applications. It achieved this success because it adapted to what its investigations and mathematics told us about the nature of matter, not what we, with our preconceived ideas, judged that reality to be.

One thing that became clear with the development of quantum theory and mechanics was that our view of the universe, and our own relationship with that universe, was something much different than had been previously imagined.

In *The Physicist's Conception of Nature*, Scientist John Wheeler writes:

> "Nothing is more important about the quantum principle than this, that it destroys the concept of the world as 'sitting out there, with the observer safely separated from it by a 20 centimeter slab of plate glass. Even to observe so miniscule an object as an electron, he must shatter the glass. He must reach in. He must install his chosen measuring equipment. It is up to him to decide whether he shall measure position or momentum. To install the equipment to measure the one prevents and excludes his installing the equipment to measure the other. Moreover, the measurement changes the state of the electron. The universe will never afterwards be the same. To describe what has happened, one has to cross out the old word 'observer' and put in its place the new word 'participator'. In some strange sense the universe is a participatory universe."

Author Fritjof Capra, in *The Tao of Physics*, writes in a similar vein:

> "Quantum theory has thus demolished the classical concepts of solid objects and of strictly deterministic laws of nature. At the subatomic level, the solid material objects of classical physics dissolve into wave-like patterns of probabilities, and these patterns, ultimately do not represent probabilities of things, but rather probabilities of interconnections.
>
> "Quantum theory thus reveals a basic oneness of the

> universe. It shows that we cannot decompose the world into independently existing smallest units. As we penetrate into matter, nature does not show us any isolated basic building blocks but rather appears as a complicated web of relations between the various parts of the whole. These relations always include the observer in an essential way. The human observer constitutes the final link in the chain of observational processes, and the properties of any atomic object can only be understood in terms of the object's interaction with the observer. This means that the classical ideal of an objective description of nature is no longer valid. The Cartesian partition between the I and the world, between the observer and the observed, cannot be made when dealing with atomic matter."

What emerges is a world vastly different from the one we are used to perceiving. We are conditioned, especially in the western, Judeo-Christian world, to see our own uniqueness and individuality as the pivotal reality in this universe. This has been the thrust of western religion and philosophy for centuries. The result has been increasing isolation and fracturing of relationships. What if this individuality and separateness is actually a mirage? What if we are not separate, but are actually linked all to all in a profound wholeness? This creates an enormous shift then in the way we begin to look at the world, at ourselves, at our actions; and this shift in perception has enormous implications. For as we perceive, so do we think and believe, and as we think and believe, so do we act. And, again, if our perception of reality is fundamentally incorrect and mistaken, we will think and act incorrectly, bringing ourselves and others unhappiness and suffering.

This way of thinking, of separating ourselves from everything in our environment, is extraordinarily deeply ingrained in our lives.

It results in enormous violence, violence that is very often triggered by the one thing that should facilitate an understanding of our common humanity - religion.

Look at the violence in the Middle East, of Northern Ireland, of the centuries old struggle between Muslims and Hindus in India.

These conflicts involve the dominant religions in the world. Why have the adherents of each of these religions been talking peace and brotherhood for thousands of years, and still not one inch of progress seems to have been made? Why do we hate each other so violently? Because we see only the differences that divide us, and cannot find the common ground of our humanity.

The Buddha, two thousand five hundred years earlier, was quoted as saying:

> "I perceived a single, invisible arrow piercing the hearts of the people."

The arrow was the delusion of difference. To the Buddha's penetrating gaze, it was clear that the underlying cause of much of the world's misery and conflict was attachment to differences, such as ethnicity and nationality, and - most ironically - differences of religion.

We can love God. We can worship God's divinity. But so often, in our own minds, we conceive of God as *separate* from people. This is why we can kill millions of people in wars. We can love God, but kill people, because people are *separate* from God, and they are *separate from us*. Whatever is different from us - *outside* of us - is the *other*. In the name of God, we can kill the enemy - the *other*.

This underlying religious outlook - the way we look at things - is constantly fracturing the world about us into separate entities. We see things in terms of us and them, black and white, good and bad, God and the Devil; and this view demonizes other people, other religions, other beliefs, other cultures, and polarizes our politics.

Science itself is telling us that the mindset that sees a distinction between oneself and what seems out there and beyond oneself is an illusion. Everything and everyone is interconnected. Buddhism views things from a similar perspective.

Buddhism sees all life as possessing the Buddha nature. There is no transcendent, anthropomorphic God sitting on high who controls things. God is within. Jesus himself said the kingdom of heaven is within. Buddha is within. Buddha is life. Life is precious. Each human being is precious because he or she possesses within his or her own life the potential for the highest state of life, that which Buddhism calls Buddhahood. To deny that in anyone is a slander and evil. Similarly, to deny the greatness of one's own life is a slander and evil.

Have you ever seen a hologram?

Holograms are three-dimensional light images. They are created by recording onto a plate the interference patterns of the wave field of light of an object - say an apple - and then illuminating that pattern with a laser beam.

Imagine a few pebbles dropped into a shallow pan of water. The ripples created by the pebbles criss-cross one another. If we were to quick-freeze the surface ripples, we would have a record of the interference pattern made by the waves. We similarly record the interference patterns of light waves from the apple, and then illuminate them with the laser beam, creating a lifelike three-dimensional image.

An extraordinary property of a hologram is that any part of it contains the whole. This means that if we illuminate any part of a hologram - say, of an apple - an image of the entire apple appears. No matter how small the part, it always contains the whole.

Holograms are not just an isolated phenomena. Holograms actually tell us something extraordinary about our own reality. We are part of the whole. Even more amazing, in some strange way, we *are* the whole. Each human being is not only part of the entire universe, but in a very real and profound way, actually is synonymous with the entirety of the universe.

Later, we will return to this idea. For the moment, however, let's turn to a central topic of this book - death - and examine how different people and cultures look at it.

chapter

4

VIEWS OF LIFE & DEATH. KARMA.

So how has Western civilization traditionally viewed life and death?

From the Western viewpoint, which is to a great extent the Judeo/Christian viewpoint, we tend to view life as beginning with birth and ending with death. What we call life is the period between those two events. What we call death is beyond those parameters. We are born, mature, and eventually die. Whatever we can aspire to, whatever we can achieve, has to take place within that time frame. There is no second chance. This is not the view of all Christians, but it is certainly the dominant historical perspective.

According to Christianity, the body perishes at death, but the soul survives. The soul only comes into being at birth, but survives death, and continues on eternally in hell or heaven, depending upon the person's faith or good works, or lack thereof, or grace, or relationship, in some fashion or other, with God.

What is heaven? It exists somewhere, where we can experience eternal happiness. What does this happiness consist of? If you ask a thousand people, they might give you a thousand different answers. Most people long to be united with their loved ones. Many wish to see justice done, the good rewarded, evil punished. And what does one do for an eternity in heaven? There are no definitive answers.

For most Christians, at death we are either saved or damned. Eternally. That's it. And for most Christians, to be saved means we accept God or Jesus as our Savior. And if we do that, even if it is on our death bed, we will be saved, and join God and Jesus in heaven.

Historically, Christianity believes men and women are born in sin. Humanity is inherently laden down with original sin, which goes back to Adam and Eve in the Garden of Eden, and Eve eating of the forbidden fruit, and obtaining knowledge. From that moment, humankind was cursed. In essence, Christianity says, we are all basically unworthy. There is something wrong with us, that we cannot solve ourselves. That's why Jesus, the son of God, was born as a human being, so that he might suffer and die for our sins, and in so doing, open up the way for our salvation. If we believe in Him, then we will be saved. And only by believing in Him, can we find salvation. It is beyond our own power to find salvation.

So basically, from the Christian viewpoint, we have this one lifetime, this one chance, to get things right. Why are we here in the first place? Why do we suffer? What is the meaning of this world, with its treachery and murder and starving and wars and unbelievable injustice. What is the meaning of millions of children dying because of lack of food or war or neglect or disease? Look at this past century, from beginning to end, with its unbelievable slaughter and death and misery, and attempt to make sense of it from a religious point of view, from a view of a just and merciful God.

A few years ago, I came to know an older Mexican-American woman who had raised a large family and had a good job in government. She was raised Catholic and raised her family in the same faith. But she told me that after the second world war, she abandoned her faith in the Church and in God, because she could find no sense or meaning to what she had experienced and witnessed. She could not have faith in a deity that allowed such atrocities to take place.

Are these horrors the workings of a just God? Why do we suffer?

Long ago, this was the question posed by Job in the Bible.

God took everything from Job - family, material wealth, health - to test his faith. At the beginning, Job cursed his own life.

> "I loathe my life; I will give free utterance to my complaint; I will speak in the bitterness of my soul."

He questioned God:

> "Does it seem good to you to oppress, to despise the work of your hands and favor the schemes of the wicked?"

In the end, Job finds his answer in submission to the power and omnipotence of God.

There have been countless attempts to explain away Job's question; but still, to our reason, as well as to our most secret heart, there seems no satisfactory answer. These eternal questions remain as real and unanswered now as they were then. Why do we suffer? What is the meaning of it all?

In 1859, a scientific work was published that was to have an extraordinarily profound effect upon the way people thought about themselves and the world in which they lived. The book was *The Origin of Species* by Charles Darwin.

From 1831 to 1836, Darwin served as a naturalist on the surveying expedition of the HMS Beagle. He visited the Cape Verde Islands, Brazil, Chile, the Galapagos Islands, Tahiti, New Zealand and Tasmania. During these five years, he obtained first-hand knowledge of the fauna, flora, and geology of these different lands. His observations caused him to reflect deeply on the problem of the origin of species. How did different species come into existence?

According to the Bible and Genesis, the world and its creatures were created out of nothing by the divine power of God.

But Charles Darwin looked at nature and came to different conclusions. He saw a world of organic evolution, in which plants and animals slowly evolved through adaptation to their changing conditions. The means by which they evolved was the process of natural selection. Those who adapted best to changing circumstances survived, and thus were favored in the reproductive process. It was the survival of the fittest that determined the evolution of species.

There was no need in Darwin's world for divine intervention, nor was mankind placed in a position of superiority versus the rest of the animal world. Darwin saw man as part of a continuum with the rest of nature, not separated by divine injunction. The logical step was to apply his discoveries and theories to humankind itself. And he did just that. In 1871, he published his Descent of Man, which laid out his theory that men and women had actually evolved from apes.

Darwin's works created both enormous interest and opposition. There was great opposition from the clergy, who realized that his theory of evolution was inconsistent with a literal interpretation of the book of Genesis. People felt threatened by the suggestion that natural laws applied to human beings just as much as they did to the world of inanimate matter. One of the most famous trials ever was the Scopes trial, brought against a Kentucky school teacher for teaching the principles of evolution - a case that was fought out between the great figures of Clarence Darrow, for the defense, and William Jennings Bryan, for the prosecution.

There arose, more and more, this enormous tension between science and religion. Here was science postulating a natural evolution that extended throughout time and space, with modern humanity only appearing at the very end of this process. Astronomy also opened up extraordinary new vistas. The vastness of the universe, as science revealed it, seemed quite beyond our capacity to realistically grasp. All of this deflated our egos enormously. Man seems inconsequential and insignificant when viewed from the perspective of a universe ruled by the laws of natural selection - a universe containing staggering numbers of suns and stars and galaxies stretching across vast voids of time and space.

These discoveries and theories had enormous impact upon peoples' psyches. If the universe is meaningless, and we expire at the end of our short journey here, then what is the purpose of morality? We can do what we wish. There are no consequences. We may conjure up something with our reason, to somehow validate moral feelings and actions; but, try as we might, at the very core, there is no fundamental purpose for morality. It comes down to the law of the jungle. The survival of the fittest. Why should not a person live to the utmost to satisfy his or her own individual desires? Why in the world should a person not live that way? What are the consequences? There are no consequences. Death is death. It is the end. Life and everything it entails is done with.

Or even to the person who believes in religion and God, if salvation can be bought at the very last gasp of life with surrender of the personal will to God, with a cry of penitence, with remorse, how does that affect how a person lives? If nothing matters except that you die in God's grace at the very last moment of your life, what prevents you from leading your life in any way you please up until that point? Why not enjoy, why not give full vent to your desires. What does it matter *what* you do? Arguments can be advanced even in this scenario, that actions do have repercussions, but at the core, it strikes many people as empty rhetoric.

Were men and woman created by God? What is the meaning of life? What is the purpose of our existence here on this planet Earth?

These are questions that have perplexed humanity for thousands of years. Within western civilization we have turned them over and thought about them in many ways. But in general, the way we have thought about these questions has always been conditioned by fundamental, underlying assumptions - the way we fundamentally look at things.

Long before the advent of western civilization and Christianity, the various cultures and religions of India wrestled with these same eternal problems, and came up with profoundly different answers.

The eastern mind views things from a cyclical perspective. Life moves in cycles, eternally recurring. Although Christianity, Judaism, Islam, Hinduism, and Buddhism all believe in some kind of eternal life, the first three view our human life span as a linear event, occurring between the time of our birth and the time of our death. After death, comes eternal life of some sort.

To the Hindu or Buddhist, however, our life exists eternally, stretching from the infinite past on into the infinite future, lifetime after lifetime. In reality, there is no such thing as birth or death as we commonly view it. There is something else, a reality which exhibits the qualities of birth and death, yet which, in actuality, is never born and never dies.

This cyclical model is what nature reveals in the natural world. The sun rises, the sun sets; the seasons move from one to another, continually repeating; spring, summer, autumn, winter; spring, summer, autumn, winter. Winter always turns to spring. Spring never turns to winter. Life comes, life goes. Life comes, death comes; life returns. Winter, or death, always turns to life and spring.

One of the great mystical poems of Hindu literature is the Bhagavad Gita, set down in written form about 300 A.D., but part of a larger epic poem, the Mahabharata, which dates back to perhaps 800 B.C.

In the Bhagavad Gita, there is a very famous scene, when Arjuna is about to lead his followers into battle against another army led by Arjuna's relatives. On the eve of this battle, Arjuna loses heart, overwhelmed by the thought of the bloodshed about to take place. His courage wavers.

At this point, Krishna, his charioteer - the earthly incarnation of Vishnu - begins a great dialogue in which he reveals to Arjuna the true nature of life and death.

Krishna explains:

"Truly there was never a time when
I was not,
Nor thou, nor these lords of men;
And neither will there be a time when
we shall cease to be;
All of us exist from this time onward.

"He who imagines this(the embodied
one) the slayer
And he who imagines this(the embodied one) the slain,
Neither of them understands;
This(the embodied one) does not slay,
nor is it slain.

"Neither is this(the embodied one)
born nor does it die at any time,
Nor, having been, will it again come
not to be.
Birthless, eternal, perpetual, prim-
aeval,
It is not slain when the body is slain."

There is no killing, no dying; no birth and death. Our lives are immortal.

"As, after casting away worn out
garments,
A man later takes new ones,
So, after casting away worn out bodies,
The embodied one encounters other,
new ones.

"For the born, death is certain;
For the dead there is certainly birth.

Therefore, for this, inevitable in
consequence,
Thou shouldst not mourn."

Human life exists eternally, transmigrating through cycles of birth and death that repeat throughout vast stretches of time. For the Hindu, the purpose of repeated births is to perfect oneself, achieve eventual release from the cycle of birth and death, and to return to Brahma, or God.

Here Buddhism and Hinduism differ in certain respects; but upon one thing they are in agreement: Throughout these cycles of birth and death, the soul or entity continues, subject to the law of cause and effect, or karma.

Karma, originally, simply meant action. Action expresses itself through thoughts, words and deeds. Inherent in the concept of karma are the workings of cause and effect. In physics, for every action there is a reaction. In our lives, for every cause we make, there is an effect. To the easterner, this is an inescapable law of life. There are no exceptions. If you steal, you will at some future time experience poverty. If you murder someone, you will, in turn, suffer the same fate in the future. If you despise others, you yourself will be looked down upon. There is no escaping the consequences of our acts, neither in this lifetime, nor in the past.

This may seem overwhelming, that we suffer the accumulated effects of so many causes from the past. To some, this has led to despair and to a hopeless acceptance of fate. But actions can be either good or bad. Good actions, whether by thought, word, or deed, lead to good effects. So we are at all times reaping the effects, good or bad, of the seeds we have sown in the past. From a broader perspective, the concept of karma leads not to a sense of fatality, but to true liberation. For it places responsibility for our destiny completely upon ourselves. We are free at any moment to change our situation and our lives.

The concept of karma leads to a much different view of suffering than that espoused by Christianity. The answer to Job's eternal question, Why do we suffer? becomes apparent. We cause our own suffering. Whatever suffering or joy we experience are the results of causes we ourselves have made in the past. We are totally responsible for our life.

From our western way of looking at things, it seems terribly unjust that some people are born poor, while others come into this world supported by luxurious conditions; that some are handsome or beautiful, and others ugly; that some are healthy, while others, for no apparent reason, are born deformed or retarded. There appears a great inequity in the way things are initially handed out. This seems very difficult to explain because we are conditioned to view life as beginning with birth. Before birth, there is no personal history.

If you accept the causality of karma, however, these same facts become readily understandable. All of these conditions are caused by our actions - our thoughts, words, and deeds.

For each child, for example, that is born into this world in any sort of condition - rich or poor, healthy or unhealthy, talented, deformed, or beautiful - there is a history of causes that produced and preceded these results. These conditions did not just appear at birth. They were created by causes we ourselves made in lifetime after lifetime that now manifest themselves in the present child's condition at birth.

Take an example of someone like Mozart. As a young child he was creating beautiful works of music. Where did this talent come from? Viewed, again, from the western belief in the initial appearance of the person at a single, unique birth, there seems no apparent answer, other than random luck, to account for Mozart's musical genius. But viewed from the perspective of karma, there were tremendous causes made in the past - who knows how or where or over how many lifetimes -that finally culminated in the flowering of his enormous musical genius.

Karma may also be thought of as deeply-ingrained patterns in our lives. Our thoughts, words and deeds can create habitual behavior that subconsciously keeps repeating itself over and over, like a worn-out record. Like any habit, repeated over and over again, it becomes difficult to break. But, in reality, we are free at any moment to change these patterns or karma, because we are free to direct our thoughts, words and deeds in a more constructive direction. At least this is the theory, although to make changes in our lives is oftentimes exceedingly difficult.

There is no such thing as a person making some kind of cause, and there being no effect. This is not in the nature of things. Everything follows the law of cause and effect. So although we may hear of a bank robber, for example, who robs banks one after the other, and is never caught, in the true scheme of things, there is no such scenario. The bank robber is always caught, and what catches him is the law of cause and effect which, at the moment of the crime, simultaneously sets into motion the effect of that crime. Somewhere, sometime, that person, our bank robber, will suffer financially, perhaps this lifetime, perhaps another lifetime in the future, but inevitably the retribution will follow, just as an echo follows a sound.

From this perspective, we begin to view our lives much differently. If we are responsible for who we are, then there is no one else in the entire universe to blame for our suffering. It may appear that someone or something is hurting us, or obstructing our wishes and desires, but in reality, this is not so. Rather, that person or circumstance that plagues us is a product of our own doing. Because we belittled people in the past, we are now looked down on in this present existence. Because we stole from others, we are now in tight, poverty-stricken circumstances. Because we disparaged ourselves in the past in one way or another, we find ourselves in situations in which we are disparaged by others. The people or circumstances in our environment are not random at all. They are creations of our own actions. We create our own karma. It is inevitable because of the workings of the law of cause and effect.

Viewing things from this perspective, we are gradually forced - if we care at all about our own suffering - to reform our behavior. If everyone knew that the inevitable consequence of killing someone would be that they would suffer the same fate in the future, there would be no need of a police force to combat crime. Who would kill someone, or rob another person, knowing that they were actually inflicting that same crime upon their own person? A world in which the law of cause and effect was universally known would be a profoundly different place than that which we currently experience. War would appear as what it actually is - the ultimate in insanity.

People often speak of karma in either a negative or positive sense. Positive things in our life are "good karma", and unpleasant things are "bad karma". But in the truest sense, karma is neither positive or negative. It simply is. What makes it good or bad is how we handle whatever we are facing in our lives at the present moment.

Some people suffer severe setbacks or tragedies; but through squarely facing these situations, are able to develop perseverance, wisdom, growth and final victory. For them, the so-called negative situation or karma actually becomes a blessing in disguise. Others, blessed with seeming good fortune and circumstances, suffer loss from the situation. An example might be someone who wins the lottery, and uses the money to travel and lay on the beach and generally lead an indolent life, instead of challenging themselves to develop their life. In the long run, their life suffers.

The purpose of Buddhism is to develop a life condition in which life itself - no matter what our present situation - is a joy. This means developing the power to overcome and transform any situation we are facing in our lives into a benefit. In the Buddhism of Nichiren Daishonin, this power is Nam Myoho Renge Kyo; and chanting Nam Myoho Renge Kyo allows us to tap that same power within our lives.

In one of his letters, Nichiren Daishonin says:

> "Suffer what there is to suffer, enjoy what there is to enjoy. Regard both suffering and joy as facts of life and continue chanting Nam-myoho-renge-kyo, no matter what happens. Then you will experience boundless joy from the Law."

chapter

5

THE NINE CONSCIOUSNESSES

There is a concept in Buddhism called the Nine Consciousnesses, which is an attempt to illuminate the functioning of the total entity of one's life in relation to the broader universal life underlying all phenomena.

The first six consciousnesses are ones we are readily familiar with. The five senses of sight, hearing, smell, taste and touch are our links to the external world. What then integrates this sensory input to form coherent images and decisions is the sixth consciousness.

The seventh consciousness is called the mano consciousness. The word mano derives from the Sanskrit word manas, meaning mind, intellect or thought, and this consciousness owes its name to the fact that it performs the act of thinking. The mano consciousness operates from within, independently of any external circumstances. It represents the realm of abstract thought, and the power to reflect upon ourselves and form judgments and the ability to grasp the underlying truth of things.

In "Unlocking the Mysteries of Birth and Death: Buddhism in the Contemporary World", Daisaku Ikeda, the current third president of the Soka Gakkai, writes:

"Another characteristic of the mano-consciousness is a

> strong attachment to the self; indeed, in addition to abstract thought and reflection, the basic function of this consciousness is that of attachment to one's own ego. Therefore the mano-consciousness is said to always be accompanied by four types of illusion: illusion that the self is absolute and unchanging; illusion leading to theories that the self is absolute and unchanging; illusion that leads to conceit; and illusion that leads to self-attachment. This consciousness, therefore, has a tendency to confine us within the framework of our own egos and thereby tempt us into arrogance and egoism. In sum, while the mano-consciousness is regarded as the locus of reason, it is simultaneously regarded as being invariably defiled by illusions concerning the self."

Below the mano-consciousness, lies an even deeper layer of consciousness, the eighth level of consciousness, or alaya-consciousness. In Sanskrit, alaya means a dwelling or receptacle. In the alaya-consciousness are stored all the workings of the first seven consciousnesses. This is the storehouse of karma, where the effects of all the thoughts, words and deeds of our lives are imprinted and stored in the form of seeds of potential for the future. Here is an accumulation of all of the experiences we have stored during previous lifetimes. Subconsciously, below our conscious level of perception and understanding, this shapes who we are and what we feel and our present circumstances.

Edgar Cayce, the famous Virginia Beach psychic, appeared to tap into this level of consciousness each time he diagnosed his patients. Cayce would be given a patient to diagnose, whom he had never met before, and who was many times not even present. Cayce would fall into a sleep-like trance, and in this state would diagnose the patient's illnesses and prescribe treatments, which in many cases seemed strange, but which often turned out to be astonishingly effective.

For example, a woman came to him complaining of an illness which her doctors told her was a laceration of the stomach. Cayce told her to disregard the doctors. Instead he told her to eat half a lemon each morning, then walk as far as she could, rest, walk home, sprinkle salt on the remaining half of the lemon, eat it, then immediately drink at least two glasses of water. The doctors thought it was a joke. The woman decided to follow Cayce's suggestion. In a few weeks she reported that she was feeling fine, could walk several miles, and found her food agreeing with her.

One time, while in a trance, Cayce was asked what the source for his knowledge was, and, still in an unconscious state, he replied:

> "Edgar Cayce's mind is amenable to suggestion, the same as all other subconscious minds, but in addition thereto it has the power to interpret to the objective mind of others what it acquires from the subconscious mind of other individuals of the same kind. The subconscious mind forgets nothing. The conscious mind receives the impression from without and transfers all thought to the subconscious, where it remains even though the conscious be destroyed."

He continued describing himself in the third person, saying that his subconscious mind was in direct communication with all other subconscious minds, and was capable of interpreting the impressions received from these other minds. In this way he tapped the knowledge possessed by millions of other subconscious minds.

While in these trance-like states, Cayce was able to cast light on a patient's suffering and illness by referring to their past lives. In the alaya-consciousness, a complete record of a person's former existences was stored; and Cayce used the knowledge of these past lives to illuminate problems of the present. Because a person acted such and such a way in the past, they were now reaping exactly what they had sowed, both good and bad.

While in one of his trances, Cayce once elaborated upon this level of consciousness:

> "The subconscious, you see, is the record of all the lives of the soul, in this system and in other systems, out among the stars. It's the record we think of as being kept by the Recording Angel. It's the story of what we do with our spirit -the portion of God that is given to us for life, with the gift of individuality, or separate existence from God. Our problem is to perfect our individuality, and then we return to God. Our spirit and soul, or individuality, are joined to Him."

Carl Jung, the great Swiss psychoanalyst, coined the term "collective unconscious" to describe a similar level of consciousness. From his studies of patients and their dreams, and from his readings of fairytales and myths throughout history, he became aware of a thread of recurring images and symbols common to the experience of all cultures and all of humanity. Jung called these universal primordial images "archetypes." They were distinct from the personal unconscious, arising from the experience of the individual. The collective unconscious, rather, described a substratum in which our own individual experience touched upon and was part of the experience of the entire human race.

Daisaku Ikeda further elaborates:

"So the alaya-consciousness contains not only the individual's karma but also the karma common to his or her family and race, and even to humanity as a whole. The realm of alaya-consciousness, therefore broadly links all living beings, and in this sense it can be said to embrace the notion of the 'collective unconscious' proposed by C. G. Jung and elaborated upon in the science of depth psychology. Jung's theory was that every human being possesses the entirety of the human heritage within the recesses of his or her own psyche - that is, that each one of us shares with all our fellow humans a common psychic base, the collective unconscious.""

If what Jung and Cayce together describe is in actuality a memory and record of humanity's shared experiences, it may be that every step in our past evolution is recorded in the deepest level of our individual minds.

In this eighth level of consciousness, nothing is ever lost. Everything that has ever been exists in some form or another, in some dimension or another. In the depths of reality, each of us touches upon and is one with each and every other human being on the face of this planet, and with the life of the universe itself, throughout time and space.

From the point of view of Buddhism, life is in constant flux, with each new millisecond carrying forward the past and embodying the past, and yet also fashioning and creating the future. Our lives are ours to fashion. And if in the depths of this eighth level of consciousness, we touch upon and affect the intricate web of relations of all people, this means that what we do and think and say has a heretofore unimagined power to influence the totality of life itself.

Referring back to the example of the hologram, just as any part of a hologram, when illuminated by itself, actually embodies the entire hologram; so our individual lives not only partake of, but actually, are, in some way, the entirety of the universe.

But Buddhism posits a level of the psyche even deeper than this level of karma or the collective unconscious. Buddhism describes a ninth level of consciousness, the amala-consciousness. The Sanskrit word amala means pure, stainless, or spotless. The amala consciousness is pure and untainted by karmic effects latent in the eighth level of consciousness. It is the ultimate reality of all things, the cosmic life force and law which embodies itself in both sentient and nonsentient existences. It is the universal Buddha nature.

The goal of Buddhist practice is to tap this inherent Buddha nature, and to bring it forth from within one's life, so that it permeates and transforms and enlightens all the other eight levels of consciousness.

Nichiren Daishonin taught that this ninth level of consciousness is Nam Myoho Renge Kyo. When we repeatedly chant these words, we can activate tremendous power and wisdom from deep within our life - wisdom and power that enables us to overcome any kind of difficulty, change our life for the better, and become supremely happy.

Nichiren Daishonin stated:

> "When deluded, one is called an ordinary being, but when enlightened, one is called a Buddha. This is similar to a tarnished mirror that will shine like a jewel when polished. A mind now clouded by the illusions of the innate darkness of life is like a tarnished mirror, but when polished, it is sure to become like a clear mirror, reflecting the essential nature of phenomena and the true

> aspect of reality. Arouse deep faith, and diligently polish your mirror day and night. How should you polish it? Only by chanting Nam-myoho-renge-kyo."

Whereas Hinduism taught that individual life was perfected lifetime after lifetime over periods of unimaginable time, finally reaching a state of enlightenment or oneness with God, Buddhism teaches that each single human being already possesses a state of supreme enlightenment or Buddhahood within, and the purpose of Buddhist practice therefore is simply to reveal this inner state of life.

What is this state of Buddhahood?

Daisaku Ikeda explains:

> "In the world of today, a person in whom the Buddha nature is expressed is at first glance a man with good sense. He is a well-integrated person, with a strong sense of responsibility and strong faith, friendly toward others and able to think flexibly. Above all, he is rich in compassion, wisdom and creativity.
>
> "People in the state of Buddhahood may not seem very exceptional at first glance....Their joy is the joy of joys: an indescribable ecstasy welling up freely and spontaneously from the innermost essence of life. There is joy in living, joy in the earth, joy in the trees and flowers, joy in the faces and movements of people - everything is colored with joy. Each breath, each wave of the hand, each step brings joy and gratitude and a love for life. Birth, old age, illness, and death are no longer sufferings, but a part of the joy of living.
>
> "The light of wisdom illuminates the entire universe,

destroying the innate benighted nature of man. The life-space of the Buddha becomes united and fused with the universe. The self becomes the cosmos, and in a single instant the life-flow stretches out to encompass all that is past and all that is future. In each moment of the present, the eternal life-force of the cosmos gushes forth as a gigantic fountain of energy. In the life of Buddhahood, each present moment contains eternity, for the entire life-force of the cosmos is compressed into a single moment of existence. A person in the state of Buddhahood is hardly conscious of the passage of physical time, because his life is full and happy at each instant, as though he were experiencing the joy of living throughout eternity."

chapter

6

NEAR-DEATH EXPERIENCES. EINSTEIN. MULTIPLE DIMENSIONS. KU.

What actually happens when we die? We know the body decomposes; but what of the self - the "I" - the center of our consciousness. Is that also extinguished? Or is there a continuation?

While there is no absolute proof to corroborate a continuation of life after the cessation of the body's functions, there is a large body of experiences of people who, in one manner or another, appeared to die, and yet returned to tell tales of their sojourn beyond their physical death.

In 1975, Dr. Raymond Moody published *Life after Life*, a summary of his encounters with many people who had had near death experiences and survived to relate what they had gone through. In each case, there were striking similarities. There was no absolute pattern to their experiences, but each person's story seemed to fit into a general overall sequence of events that people experienced after they had apparently "died".

First, as Dr. Moody relates, they suddenly find themselves outside of their own physical body, and are able to watch their body from a distance, objectively, like a spectator. They become aware that they still have a body, but it is a body with different powers, existing in a different dimension. Many times, there is a feeling of traveling through a tunnel or darkness, and at the end of this, they encounter a bright light which emanates overwhelming love and compassion.

There comes a total review of their life, in the most intimate detail - yet flashing by in their mind's eye almost instantaneously. The thoughts, words and deeds of an entire lifetime are perfectly mirrored is this review. There is no judgment from the source of light, however, only immense compassion. What happens beyond this point is unknown, for each of the people recounting their experience is then drawn back, for whatever reason, into his or her physical body and returns to life in this world.

For those who have had near-death experiences, and returned to tell their tale, what was the core nature of their experience?

Dr. Moody recorded the feelings of a no-nonsense businessman who had had a near-death experience during a cardiac arrest when he was sixty-two:

> "The first thing I saw when I awoke in the hospital was a flower, and I cried. Believe it or not, I had never really seen a flower until I came back from death. One big thing I learned when I died was that we are all part of one big, living universe. If we think we can hurt another person or another living thing without hurting ourselves, we are sadly mistaken. I look at a forest or a flower or a bird now, and say, 'That is me, part of me." We are connected with all things and if we send love along those connections, then we are happy."

Another great pioneer in the investigation of the processes of dying and of near-death experiences during the 1970's and the decades beyond was Elisabeth Kubler-Ross. Kubler-Ross was formerly a professor on the psychiatric faculty of the University of Chicago. Her work brought her into contact with many terminally ill patients. Against the opposition of most of her colleagues, she began interviewing these patients and incorporating their experiences into her classroom clinical work. She found that patients moved through several stages of dying, from utter denial to final acceptance, and that a clear understanding of this process was important to clearing up unresolved feelings of patients.

In her studies of the dying process and death, she also interviewed patients who had been declared dead, but later revived. Although herself a Protestant, she did not really believe in a life after death. But after years of working with thousands of patients, she confides that she was forced to change her mind and came to realize that life goes on continuously even after death. She reports her results as follows:

> "With many of these patients, we found out that their experience is that, at the moment of physical death, they float out of their physical body and they float a few feet above the hospital bed or the accident scene. They can see themselves lying in the bed and they can distinguish many things. They can describe in minute, very fine detail who came into the room and they can describe a resuscitation attempt. They can say which doctor or nurse, which family member, which priest was in the room. They describe the color of their dress, at the time they have no vital signs.
>
> "At the first instant of death, the moment of physical separation is a good experience. Like getting out of a prison. What Christians call 'hell', heaven or hell, the difference between good people and bad people, people who have led very enlightened lives and those who have not, comes afterwards, after separation. What Christians

call 'hell' is not as Christians describe it.

"After they leave, they go through the walls - they don't need an open door or window - and then they go toward a light, through a tunnel, over a bridge or river. After they have passed over, then comes what a Christian would call 'hell'. There is no god who condemns you, but you are forced to review your own life.

"It's like watching a television screen and your whole life is passed in front of you, not only deeds but also thoughts. This is going through hell, because you see everything you have ever done and thought. So it is not a god who condemns you, but you condemn yourself."

Throughout the 1970's, Kubler-Ross took part in interviewing about 20,000 people who had had near-death experiences, ranging in ages from two years to ninety-nine years, and including a broad cross-spectrum of people from vastly diverse cultures. In all cases, the experiences were so similar that she felt the accounts had to be true. She writes:

"Up till then I had absolutely no belief in an afterlife, but the data convinced me that these were not coincidences or hallucinations."

Carl Jung, himself, had an extraordinary near-death experience when he was about seventy, in connection with an accident. He writes:

"I can describe the experience only as the ecstasy of a non-temporal state in which present, past and future are one. Everything that happens in time had been brought together into a concrete whole. Nothing was distributed over time, nothing could be measured by temporal con-

> cepts. One is interwoven into an indescribeable whole yet observes it with complete objectivity."

From his own experiences and dreams, and from work with his patients, Jung became convinced that our normal ideas of space and time were incomplete. He stated:

> "There are indications that at least a part of the psyche is not subject to the laws of space and time. Scientific proof of that has been provided by the well-known J. B. Rhine experiments. Along with numerous cases of spontaneous fore-knowledge, non-spatial perceptions, and so on - of which I have given a number of examples from my own life - these experiments prove that the psyche at times functions outside of the spatio-temporal law of causality. This indicates that our conceptions of space and time, and therefore of causality also, are incomplete. A complete picture of the world would require the addition of still another dimension; only then could the totality of phenomena be given a unified explanation. Hence it is that the rationalists insist to this day that parapsychological experiences do not really exist; for their world-view stands or falls by this question. If such phenomena occur at all, the rationalistic picture is invalid, because incomplete. Then the possibility of an other-valued reality behind the phenomenal world becomes an inescapable problem, and we must face the fact that our world, with its time, space, and causality, relates to another order of things lying behind or beneath it, in which neither 'here and there' nor 'earlier and later' are of importance. I have been convinced that at least a part of our psychic existence is characterized by a relativity of space and time. This relativity seems to increase, in proportion to the distance from consciousness, to an absolute condition of timelessness and spacelessness."

In the early years of the twentieth century, science was verging upon similar conclusions.

In 1905, Albert Einstein published his famous Special Theory of Relativity. His theory grew out of the results of an experiment that had taken place in 1887 in Cleveland, Ohio.

Scientists Albert Michelson and Williams Morley had set up an experiment to measure the speed of the earth in absolute space. Their actual intent, however was to prove the existence of the ether, which at that time was widely believed to be an invisible substance filling all of the universe.

The experiment involved sending out light beams in two directions, perpendicular to each other, which were then reflected back to the source by mirrors placed identical distances from the light source. Light travels at enormous speed, but the measuring instruments the two men used were precise enough to measure minute discrepancies in time. The ether was never proven; but an astonishing side fact emerged from this experiment. When measurements were taken of the round-trip time intervals of the two beams of light, they were found to be precisely identical. Since one of the directions of light coincided with the forward motion of the earth, while the other was perpendicular to it, one would suppose that the times elapsed for the beams of light to return to their source would be different. But this was not the case. The Michelson-Morley experiment seemed to indicate that the speed of light was absolute.

This contradicts all of our common-sense notions of speed. For instance, if we are travelling in a car going 50 miles and hour and are passed by another car going 70 miles an hour, the speed of the second car, relative to our own, would be 20 miles an hour. If, on the other hand, another car approached us from the opposite direction that we were heading in, and the speed of this car was again 70 miles an hour, the second car, relative to our own, would seem to be travelling much faster than the car approaching us from the rear.

However, the Michelson-Morley experiment said that, when considering light, these observations do not hold. Whether an observer is moving or at rest, the speed of light is always the same. The speed of light is absolute.

Scientists were baffled by the results of the experiment. Michelson himself spent a great deal of time searching for mistakes in his calculations. But there were none. The result was always the same. The speed of light was absolute.

Einstein's approach to this problem, however, was to take the results of the Michelson-Morley experiment at face value. His special theory of relativity was based on two fundamental suppositions: First, that all true laws of physics are absolute, and, second, that the speed of light is absolute. From these two postulates, he developed his entire theory of relativity.

His theory led him to conclude that space and time are not two independently existing entities, but rather two aspects of a single phenomena - space-time. Space and time are inextricably interwoven. They cannot be separated. We cannot visualize space-time; it exists in a different dimension than the three dimensional world we are used to dealing with. Space-time is a fourth dimension.

This sounds more like science fiction than pure science; and yet experiments since then have only confirmed the correctness of Einstein's theories, and opened up heretofore undreamed of possibilities - as with his famous equation, E=mc2, which was the foundation for the unleashing of atomic energy.

One of the problems which haunted Einstein during his last years was reconciling his own theories of relativity with quantum theory. The theory of relativity was great for explaining the larger workings of the universe. Quantum theory, on the other hand, obtained extraordinary results when applied to the subatomic world. But neither theory could explain both the larger universe and subatomic behavior. The two theories could not be reconciled. Einstein labored for the last part of his life to find a Unified Field Theory that could explain both phenomena. But he never found it.

Today, the most cutting-edge developments in this search for a unified theory of physics involve "string" theory. Over the past 20 or so years, this new theory has gained an increasing number of enthusiasts in the scientific community. The theory proposes that the entire universe and everything in it is made up of microscopic vibrating strings.

String theory points to a universe of multiple dimensions - in fact, more than likely, one of eleven dimensions. Exploration into the world of superstrings has been carried out solely through mathematics, so no one has ever seen these eleven dimensions - let alone the four dimensions of Einstein's space-time - but the mathematics seem to work. Scientists are coming closer than ever to a solution that unites all the various forces of physics - such as gravity, electromagnetism, electrons, etc., - into one grand, fundamental, unified law of our universe.

What or where these multiple dimensions are, we do not know. Our minds can not even comprehend what they might be. But the developing mathematics of string theory seem to point to the existence of such dimensions just as surely as Einstein's equations forced us to confront the reality of space-time.

Buddhism, in a sense, addresses this question of another dimension also, employing the concept of ku, or the Middle Way. The concept of ku was part of the theoretical foundation of Mahayana Buddhism developed by Nagarjuna, a Buddhist scholar in southern India, who is thought to have lived between A.D. 150 and 250.

Ku is a doctrine of non-substantiality, also translated as emptiness, nothingness, or void. Many people take this as a kind of negation, and look upon Buddhism therefore in a negative light. Nothing could be farther from the truth. The nothingness of ku is not what we normally think of when we think of nothingness. It means that entities have no fixed or independent nature in and of themselves. The essence of life is change, moment to moment; and all phenomena, including human life, arises and continues to exist only by virtue of relationships with other phenomena.

One might liken our lives to waves on the ocean. Waves arise, crest, then fall back into the ocean. In the same way, our lives appear from the universe, from ku, take on an individuality, then dissolve back into ku at death. But the wave, when cresting, never exists totally by itself; nor when it subsides, does it disappear. Even as a visible wave, it is connected to the ocean and to the vastness of the entire ocean and of every other wave. It has been part of the ocean all along. When it dissolves, it simply takes on another form, a form we cannot readily observe. This is ku. It is neither existence, nor non-existence. It is neither life, nor death. It is the Middle Way. Birth and death are only two aspects of the same thing - Life itself. Life manifests itself sometimes as existence, or life, and at other times as death. But Life itself - or the ocean - never ceases to exist.

But what of our self, our identity? What happens to our self? Does it disappear? The wave seems to disappear. And what consolation is it that perhaps we merge with the larger universe, the ocean of life, if our own individuality is not retained. Where is our self in all this? Does our self disappear? Does the "I" disappear?

Buddhism sees this sense of the absolute self, or the ego, as illusion. In our egocentricity, we envision our own selves as absolute and independent of all other existences. This is the fallacy we labor under.

Just as the wave is never separate from the ocean, so we are never separate and distinct from the whole of life around us. In the same way, Jung explained that our psyches are all connected in the depths of life, in the collective unconscious.

But the question still arises, what happens to the self? This question becomes of all-critical importance when looked at from the point of view of karma. For, as some have pointed out, if the self does not survive death in an individual way, as a sort of immortal life or soul, rather than some indiscriminate merging into the whole, then how can individual karma be carried forward to a future life?

Jung, himself, formulated this essential question:

> "The idea of rebirth is inseparable from that of karma. The crucial question is whether a man's karma is personal or not. If it is, then the preordained destiny with which a man enters life represents an achievement of previous lives, and a personal continuity therefore exists. If, however, this is not so, and an impersonal karma is seized upon in the act of birth, then that karma is incarnated again without there being any personal continuity."

But in Buddhism, again, there are not simply these two options. There is the Middle Way.

In his dialogue with Dr. Bryan Wilson of All Souls College Oxford, published as *Human Values in a Changing World*, Daisaku Ikeda addresses this problem:

> "Buddhism inherited the ancient Indian concept of transmigration but enriched and developed it in distinctive ways. The Buddhist interpretation is that individual life is determined by cause-and-effect relations and that - as you have pointed out - there is no such thing as a permanently persisting ego(soul). Other religions object that if there is no soul to persist from existence to existence there can be no transmigration. The apparent inconsistency is resolved if the Buddhist position is put this way: although denying the existence of an eternal, immutable soul, Buddhism recognizes a life entity that transmigrates while changing constantly when projected as a phenomenal existence. This is to say, what transmigrates is neither John Brown nor anything that can be identified as his soul and his soul only. What persists through time is a life entity that may have been manifested an infinity of times in an infinity of circumstances, all of which have left karmic effects for better or worse on the entity itself. John Brown is only one of those karma-determined manifestations, but he, too, has made his karmic contribution."

What this implies is a possible dimension to what we call life and death that makes one pause and deeply reflect. Perhaps nothing is ever lost, in a very real sense. People who have encountered near-death experiences, died and then returned, speak of meeting loved ones who have passed on. In dreams, time and space have little meaning. The here-and-now, the future, events past and present are interwoven into a dimensionless setting. Perhaps this is our lives as they truly exist.

Is there more to this universe than meets our eyes?

The great historian Arnold Toynbee summed up his own conclusions on the subject:

> "I conclude that the phenomenon of death, followed by the disorganization of the physical aspect of a personality that we encounter as a psychosomatic unity, is, in terms of reality-in-itself, an illusion arising from the limitations of the human mind's conceptual capacity....I believe that reality itself is timeless and spaceless but that it does not exist in isolation from our time-and-space-bound world."

What is this reality? The most cutting-edge inquiries of present-day physics point to the existence of a hidden reality underlying the visible universe. The most up-to-date experiments indicate that what we see of stars and galaxies and super-galaxies - whose reach and size are staggering - is only the tip of the iceberg as to what really comprises our universe. Physicists now believe that about a third of the universe is composed of a dark matter, which is invisible and undetectable so far, from which electrons and matter are constantly being spawned. Even more startling, they now believe that almost a full two-thirds of our universe is actually some kind of dark energy, which underlies and permeates everything in our universe. Physicists know there is something there, but as to what this dark matter and dark energy actually are, they have not really a clue. They know only that whatever is there seems to be the dominant energy of the cosmos.

This energy, in Buddhism, is Nam-Myoho-Renge-Kyo. It is the underlying life and life-force of the universe itself, permeating everything.

In 1922, Carl Jung had a dream of being with his father, who had died in 1896. Jung wanted to bring his father up to date about all that had happened to him and his family since his father's death, but his father was preoccupied with other thoughts. He wanted to consult his son about marital psychology. Jung prepared to give a lecture on the subject, but then awoke. A few months later, Jung's mother died.

He writes:

> "My parents' marriage was not a happy one, but full of trials and difficulties and tests of patience. Both made the mistakes typical of many couples. My dream was a forecast of my mother's death, for here was my father who, after an absence of twenty-six years, wished to ask a psychologist about the newest insights and information on marital problems, since he would soon have to resume this relationship again. Evidently he had acquired no better understanding in his timeless state and therefore had to appeal to someone among the living who, enjoying the benefits of changed times, might have a fresh approach to the whole thing...Such was the dream's message."

Rather than the dead knowing more than the living, Jung was led to believe the very reverse is true: the dead depend upon the living for any further development of their own knowledge and consciousness.

Again Jung observes:

> "The maximum awareness which has been attained anywhere forms, so it seems to me, the upper limit of knowledge to which the dead can attain. That is probably why earthly life is of such great significance, and why it is that

> what a human being 'brings over' at the time of his death is so important. Only here, in life on earth, where the opposites clash together, can the general level of consciousness be raised. That seems to be man's metaphysical task."

Referring back to Tolstoy's *Death of Ivan Ilyitch*, which we talked about at the beginning of this book, we find Ivan Ilyitch continuing to struggle on his deathbed through intense pain and despair to get at the meaning of his life.

> "For three straight days, during which time did not exist for him, he struggled in that black sack into which he was being thrust by an unseen, irresistable force. He struggled as a man condemned to death fights in the hands of an executioner, knowing that he cannot save himself. And every moment he felt that, despite all his struggles, he was drawing nearer and nearer to what terrified him. He felt he was in agony because he was being thrust into that black hole, but, at the same time, was not able to get right into it. What prevented him from getting into it was his belief that his life had been good. This very justification of his life held him fast and prevented him from advancing, and caused him more agony than anything else.
>
> "Suddenly some force struck him in the chest and side, making it still harder to breathe; he fell through the hole and there at the bottom was a light....
>
> "This took place at the end of the third day, an hour before his death. Just then his schoolboy son had crept into the room and gone up to his father's bedside. The dying man was still screaming desperately and waving his arms. His hand fell on the child's head. The boy

seized it, pressed it to his lips and began to cry.

"At that very moment Ivan Ilyich fell through the hole and caught sight of the light, and it was revealed to him that his life had not been what it ought to have been but that it was still possible to put it right. 'But what *is* the right thing?' he asked himself, and grew still, listening. Just then he felt someone kissing his hand. He opened his eyes and looked at his son. He felt sorry for him. His wife came up to him, and he looked at her. She was gazing at him with open mouth, with unwiped tears on her nose and cheeks, and a look of despair on her face. He felt sorry for her....

"And suddenly it became clear to him that what had been oppressing him and would not go away was now dropping away on one side, on two sides, on ten sides, on all sides. He felt sorry for them, he wanted to do something for them, to release them and himself from this suffering. 'How good and how simple,' he thought. 'And the pain?' he asked himself. 'Where has it gone? Where are you, pain?'

He began to look for it.

'Yes, here it is. Well, what of it? Let it be.'

'And death? Where is it?'

He searched for his accustomed fear of death and did not find it. 'Where is it? What death?' There was no fear because there was no death.

Instead of death there was light.

> 'So that's it!' he exclaimed. 'What joy!'
>
> All this happened in a single moment, and the meaning of that moment did not change thereafter. For those present his agony continued another two hours. Something rattled in his throat, and his emaciated body twitched. Then the gasping and rattle became less frequent.
>
> 'It is all over!' said someone near him.
>
> He heard the words and repeated them in his soul. 'Death is over,' he said to himself. 'It is no more.'
>
> He drew in a breath, stopped in the middle of it, stretched out and died."

With the meeting of the light, a new dimension unfolds within the mind and soul of Ivan Ilyitch - one filled with compassion and the eternity of life.

This moving fictionalized account is so similar to the actual experiences recounted by those who have gone through near-death experiences - an encounter with the light, and the sense of extraordinary compassion emanating from it.

What is this light?

Some feel it is a religious figure, like Christ or Buddha. But in his book, "Life at Death: A Scientific Investigation of the Near-Death Experience," Dr. Kenneth Ring examined in detail the stories of 102 people who had near-death experiences and was able to show that religion is no more a factor in the near-death experience than race or age.

He also stated the conclusion his investigations had led him to:

The objective detachment from the body, the sense of a different dimension of space and time, the travel down a dark space or tunnel, were indications, for Dr. Ring, of a dramatic shift in consciousness.

> "My own interpretation rests on the assumption that these experiences reflect psychological events associated with a shift in levels of consciousness. The intermediate states of the core experience can be understood as initiating a transition from a state of consciousness rooted in 'this-world' sensory impressions to one that is sensitive to the realities of another dimension of existence."

But his most astonishing conclusion then follows:

> "The next phenomenon that manifests itself is, of course, the brilliant golden light, which is sometimes seen at the end of the tunnel and at other times appears independent of a tunnel experience. Sometimes, as we have noted, people report that it envelops them rather than being seen as though at a distance.
>
> "I submit that this presence/voice is actually - oneself! It is not merely a projection of one's personality, however, but one's total self, or what in some traditions is called the higher self.
>
> "In this view, the individual personality is but a split-off fragment of the total self with which it is reunited at the point of death. During ordinary life, the individual personality functions in a seemingly autonomous way, as though it were a separate entity. In fact, however, it is invisibly tied to the larger self structure of which it is a part.

> "What has this to do with the light? The answer is - or so I would say - that this higher self is so awesome, so overwhelming, so loving, and unconditionally accepting (like an all-forgiving mother) and so foreign to one's individualized consciousness that one perceives it as separate from oneself, as unmistakably other. It manifests itself as a brilliant golden light, but it is actually oneself, in a higher form, that one is seeing. It is as though the individual, being thoroughly identified with his own limited personality, asks: 'What is that beautiful light over there?', never conceiving for a moment that anything so magnificent could possibly be himself in his complete - we need to add here, divine - manifestation. The golden light is actually a reflection of one's own inherent divine nature and symbolizes the higher self. The light one sees, then, is one's own.
>
> "The higher self, furthermore, has total knowledge of the individual personality, both past and future. That is why, when it is experienced as a voice, it seems to be an 'all-knowing' one. That is why it can initiate a life review, and, in addition, provide a preview of an individual's life events. At this level, information is stored holographically and experienced holographically - simultaneously or nearly so."

In Buddhism, this higher self is called Nam Myoho Renge Kyo, the essence of our own life and of everything else in the universe. It is the Buddha nature, inherent in all life. Nichiren Daishonin, in the 13th century, perceived and became enlightened to this law within his own life, and began the chanting of Nam Myoho Renge Kyo to enable any person, regardless of status, intelligence, race, or gender to awaken the power of the Buddha nature within his or her own life. This was not an intellectual or mental exercise, but rather a direct way of connecting one's individual life to the greater life of the universe itself, which, in essence, as Dr. Ring so movingly describes, is actually one's own greater self.

By doing this, a person is able to connect their individual life to the rhythm and power of the universe itself, enabling that person to call forth the wisdom, courage, hope, compassion, and great fortune already inherent within their own life. In so doing, any person can bring forth the life force which will enable them to change even the deepest karma within his or her life. Karma resides on the eighth level of consciousness, but Nam Myoho Renge Kyo is itself the ninth level of consciousness, which, once activated, floods upwards to influence and enlighten all the other levels of our life. The result is positive change and immense benefit and happiness.

Daisaku Ikeda writes:

> "...all forms of life in the universe, regardless of their temporal condition, are essentially directed to the Buddha nature. In other words, the most fundamental urge in life is an aspiration for Buddhahood -the impulse to combine with the cosmic life-force and to return to its essence. This urge, which is stronger than love, hate, reason, desire, or even the wish to live, is at the innermost core of each individual life, and often it is veiled by the workings of desire and ignorance. Still it is there, in all beings, and it is the most basic human craving of all. I call it *religious desire*, or the *instinct for the ultimate truth*.
>
> "In the religion of Nichiren Daishonin, every person can become a complete realization of the Buddhahood within his own self."

LIFE & DEATH PANEL DISCUSSION

The following panel discussion, with questions also from the audience, was held July 29, 2000 in Los Angeles at the SGI Friendship Center. The participants on the panel were, in alphabetical order:

Margie Hall
Eric Hauber
Theresa Hauber
Shinji Ishibashi

Shinji Ishibashi

What I am going to start off with is a very theoretical explanation; but I hope this will set the tone for what we are going to discuss in the rest of this panel discussion.

Very simply put, Buddhism believes we have lived forever, and we shall live forever. In this Buddhist view, Buddhism looks at the universe as a vast living entity itself. In it, the individual life goes through the cycle of life and death. We experience this every day, the universe being a big living entity, and each individual life going in and out. In our body every day millions of cells, out of say 60 trillion cells in our body, die and are reborn through the metabolic system. So the fundamental life force that exists within this sentient body returns to the wholeness of the universe. In other words, it is never created and never dies. It never disappears, it's always there.

Nichiren Daishonin also wrote on this perspective:

> "When we examine the nature of life with the perfect enlightenment, we find that there is no beginning marking birth, therefore no end signifying death."

So life and death are considered as the two essential phases of life. Both of them are very important. Just as we go to sleep to refresh our self and replenish our energy for the next day, the sleep cycle and the death cycle are the same, just different in length.

In the 5th century A.D., the Indian scholar Vasabandhu, a very famous scholar in Buddhism, came up with the nine consciousness teaching, in which he described life. We gather information from the first five layers of consciousness or senses that we have - feeling it, smelling it, seeing it, hearing it, tasting it. The sixth layer of consciousness, the conscious mind comes up with tangible judgments. For instance, a big truck is coming down a hill and you are on the bicycle. You look at the size and width of the street, and you decide, oh, oh, this is too narrow, so you go to the side and let the truck pass by. That's a very tangible, logical decision, and example of the process of the sixth level of consciousness.

Then there is the seventh level of consciousness, what we call the subconscious mind. Freud is a well known proponent of this level of consciousness. This is where the profound sense of self resides - things like personality or sense of being. There we make intangible decisions - decisions such as good and bad.

Then there is the eighth level of consciousness, where potential energy and karma resides. This is where the potential energy created by our deeds - thoughts, words, and actions, good and bad - is stored; and when the time comes, these manifest in physical form. This is an interesting conscious level. This is where our profound life tendency exists. Our life tendency itself is karma.

Buddhism does not consider this karma to be fixed or unchangeable. Rather it can be changed. What makes it so difficult to change is our life tendency that we have built over several lifetimes. This eighth level of consciousness interacts with the other levels of consciousnesses, and this is where we, as human beings, exert influence upon one another, on our surroundings, and upon all life.

We know we should not be jealous of anyone. We know we should be magnanimous and supportive of everyone. When it comes right down to it, though, that person right next to you has to be an exception - right? All the things they did to me. And we come up with wonderful reasons to denounce that person, but the bottom line could really be jealousy or envy of the wonderful quality that person has. We cannot bear to be inferior to that person, and try to drag that person down. And this tendency is so strong, knowing that we should not do that, we cannot help it. We cannot help it so much so, that we delude ourselves into thinking that we are not even doing it. We have a wonderful reason for whatever we do.

I'm sorry, I see strange expressions in your faces. I think I'm speaking to the wrong crowd. You are not guilty of this at all. But this is the way human beings are - outside of this room.

This is the level where the actual cycle of life and death takes place. There is a balance sheet. Do you know what the balance sheet is in your karma? Good and bad. Creative and destructive. Selfishness and altruism. All of these things we create. And however we live out this life, after that there's a balance sheet that determines the circumstances in which we will be born. So this continuation is so strict.

Now if we really understood some of the things we do, knowingly or unknowingly, creating a very specific manifested effect, I don't think we would do some of the things we do. But we don't understand - we don't have an awareness of it, that's why we do it. But there's a strictness to it. The karma is very much fixed, in the sense of our unwillingness to challenge ourselves, to make the cause at this very moment, and if we have the courage to face who we are, and are willing to go against that life tendency, and make the cause that dynamically reshapes the future, we can do so. That's where the real meaning of life is.

Then there's the last one - the ninth level of consciousness, which is the deepest conscious level which we possess inside. It is the very source of cosmic life. It is an undefiled life condition, free from the karmic flow. It is the pureness called wisdom or mercy. We have that life condition and our challenge in our practice of Buddhism is to tap that, awaken to that. Then that will interact with the eighth level of consciousness, the storehouse of karma we call it. Awakening to that ninth level of consciousness called enlightenment or Buddhahood or wisdom will directly work on the eighth level of consciousness, the layer of karma, thereby transforming that into the shallower layer of expression, thus making it changeable. This is our practice.

PANEL DISCUSSION

Eric Hauber

President Ikeda said once that even if we understand all the theory, it still doesn't necessarily mean we have a joyful life. So part of what we would like to do is to begin to talk about the reality of life and death, particularly as it affects us and also people we know, and try to put what Shinji talked about into a more everyday thing.

In particular, what I would like to start with is, we all have assumptions about death, whether we are aware of it or not, and these assumptions color how we look at living, life, taking chances, falling in love, falling out of love. For instance, if I asked you this question, when you think of death, what color do you think of. Black, right? If you think of death, does the word joy or suffering come to mind? Suffering, right? So who wants to deal with death? Because our conception of death is heavy. It assumes suffering. And we look at it as extinction.

When you say life and death, they are opposites in our mind; so that death becomes the extinction of life. But in actuality, from a Buddhist perspective, birth and death are the phases of life; and we transit through these phases just as naturally as anything. President Ikeda once asked: Whoever said that death is painful? I think he was talking about we who chant Nam Myoho Renge Kyo who have no fear of death - not because we have talked ourselves into it, but because we have an awareness from our own experience of what life is, and therefore death is a part of that. If you just simply look around us outside, we see that people talk about the birth of stars; we talk about the death of stars; we talk about the beginnings of the universe. You watch trees go through the cycle of death in which the leaves fall off, they go through a time of refreshing, and then in the springtime they are reborn again. Everything we see around us does this. Why are we the only elements of life that don't do this? A

Buddhist perspective is: we aren't. To be alive is to go through the cycles of birth and death. Our delusion is that death is suffering , or that death is an extinction of life.

Honestly speaking, none of us are experts on death. None of us remember the last one we had. And we are also somewhat afraid of the next one coming up. But the saving grace in all of this, from a Buddhist perspective, is that we are all becoming experts on how to live life. What we have not caught up to yet is that becoming an expert on how to live life is at the same time becoming an expert on how to experience a wonderful, joyful death.

Theresa Hauber:

I'm going to talk primarily from experience in dealing with this issue professionally. I've had the experience of working with the elderly, as I do right now, but have also helped put into place some legislation and policy about peoples' choice - being able to choose what type of quality of life they would like to have, especially at the end of life.

As a society overall, for those of us here in the United States of America and in western culture, it's not our favorite topic. We do not want to talk about it. We would like to avoid it as much as possible. And it's been shown statistically that the last year of life is the most costly. For several reasons: it's because we want to continue to live for absolutely as long as possible and we'll do anything - absolutely anything - to prolong it, even for one more month, or even for one more day. And often that happens because maybe even a person who is quite ready to move on to their next phase of life has family members who are not willing to help them do that, for whatever reason. It could be because of issues they've had, or wanting to do absolutely anything and everything - so that they don't have any guilt feelings at the end - of having done their utmost to help their relative or parent or whoever it is. So this issue of death is very difficult, not only for individuals, but for society as a whole. We have made a lot of progress however. We're beginning to educate ourselves quite a bit. We're beginning to hold dialogues about it - about what quality of life do I want to have at the last stage of life. And about having the ability to make a choice.

We're now beginning to say that it is our right; and we're also beginning to say that it's an ethical decision as to who is making that decision, and giving consent to many things. So in that regard, we're making a lot of progress. And in this vein, this Buddhism is incredibly valuable, not only for us as practicing Buddhists, wanting to create this fantastic karma that we are going to take with us, but also for those who are not chanting and who are not Buddhists.

Everyone and everything has Nam Myoho Renge Kyo. Life itself is Nam Myoho Renge Kyo. So there is nothing we see, the book, the flower, our life, that doesn't have Nam Myoho Renge Kyo. Some of us are aware of it because we have been introduced to it, and we know how to stimulate and bring out a higher life condition.

So one of my experiences was how I was able to share this philosophy with someone who knew nothing about it, especially at the end of their life.

I am a home health nurse and one evening I was at dinner and my little beeper went off, and I made the call, and a woman on the other end said "Come quick, come quick. My mother's dying." I asked, did you know your mother was going to die?, and she replied that, yes, we knew she was going to die.

"And you chose to keep her at home?"

"Yes, we chose to keep her at home."

So I told her that there was nothing I could do clinically that was going to make a difference. But she said, "No, no, no, you come".

So I went there. It was back east, and it was cold, and I pulled up to the house and it was really dark, and I walked in, and the living room was really dark. They showed me through to a room where this lady was lying in bed, and all around were all of her adult children, and they're just sitting there, asking, "What are we going to do?" I took the lady's blood pressure, and of course it was completely flat at that moment, but I didn't really want to tell them because they were very concerned. They asked, "What is it, what is it?" and I said, "Well, it's very normal - for the circumstances."

They said, "What are we going to do - shall we whisk her to the hospital?"

I thought to myself: I'm a Buddhist. Am I going to tell them to chant Nam Myoho Renge Kyo and your mom's going to get better? I thought, no I can't do that. But I can somehow, based on my perspective about what life is, perhaps help them through this difficult time.

So I told them:

"Look, she must have been a very grand lady. She must have been stupendous. Life is cause and effect. A person who has not had a glorious life, or has not been a glorious mother, isn't going to be lying in her own bed, having every single one of her children and her husband around her. She must have been one wonderful lady."

This is based on our position that life is cause and effect. This was the effect of the tremendous causes she had made.

The woman said, “Yes, she was a great lady”.

I said, “Listen, this is what you do. You sit down, all four of you. You sit around this bed, and even though she looks like she’s not responding, she can hear everything you say. So I want you to tell her all of the grand things that she did, what a wonderful lady she was, and how much you appreciate and love her, and I want you to wish her the best.”

So they said they would. Then I told them to call me if they needed anything, and left.

About three o’clock in the morning, the phone rang, and the woman said, “Come quick, come quick! She died!” So I said okay and went right over there, and you should have seen - the lights were on, the coffee was there, the sweet rolls were there.

They said, “Come see! Come take a look at her!”

This lady who had died was smiling, she was pink, and she was even warmer than when I was there the first time. It’s the truth! And I felt so appreciative that I had run across this tremendous philosophy of True Buddhism, and that we have this opportunity to live our lives based on cause and effect.

The other experience that I want to share is my own. I had gotten to a certain crossroads of my life, when my children were suddenly grown and gone, and I suddenly had no plan for the rest of my life.

I sat down and began to chant about this, and the first thing that came out through my wisdom was the thought: “What if you were on your deathbed. What would make you say that you had led a very satisfying life?" And from that moment I began to think: What would make me say I had led a very satisfying life? I would like you to try it - it has a very profound effect. I had to completely shift my gears. Nothing I was doing on that day when I began to chant that way was going to get me to what I thought was going to lead to a satisfying life. In fact, quite the opposite. So the point is, Nichiren Daishonin says first accept death and then live the rest of your life after that, and I really began to understand that.

Margie Hall:

I would like to share from the perspective of a child growing up with this practice. Next year I am going to be celebrating my fortieth year of practice. My sisters were 5 and 7, and I was 9 when I first started chanting Nam Myoho Renge Kyo. Two weeks ago I returned from visiting my mother in Okinawa. I had not been back in 24 years. We always met in Hawaii, because that's where the rest of my family lives. When we were together during those two weeks, we had all these great family talks. We were sitting around the dining table, and we were talking about the fact that if any of us were to drop dead at that moment, we would have no regrets. We have all overcome innumerable obstacles and have truly lived a very fulfilling life. That's what we all felt, my sisters, my nieces, my mother.

When I think about the subject of death, I was a child when my grandfather died - my mother's father. At that time I was living in Okinawa and his body was placed in a coffin in front of the altar for a few days. That was the custom in that town. My sisters and I and my father were there. My father led us to the coffin, and we sat around the coffin. That was my first exposure to someone who had died. He was sleeping, like a baby. My father told me to touch him because I needed to experience what this practice does for someone who dies.

My father told me they go into a sleep, a deep sleep, and then, when they're ready, their life wakes up again. So I felt his body and it was cold; but the impact of that first impression of death was so deep in my life. I thought: That's what people do when they die. Of course, along the way, I learned about cause and effect and all the theories of Buddhism, but that first exposure to death was a great one.

And then my father died. He died of a heart attack at work. I was in Hawaii at the time, and my sisters and I flew back to Okinawa. What we experienced, once again, was the most amazing thing. The funeral was really grand. The following day, we went to the crematorium, and I'll never forget it. As the oldest child in the family, I was given the torch to light up the crematorium. I'll never forget the image. A few yards away was this other crematorium, and this young girl about 20 years old was screaming - screaming in deep, deep anguish, calling for her mother - "Why did you have to leave me here alone!" She was screaming in a ghastly manner, and the three of us, especially my little sister, were just scared to death, just listening to this woman screaming, because we were so at peace, just waving goodbye to our father, because we knew he would be reborn. That was our belief system.

Reuniting in the last month, we recounted all these episodes, and what we had gone through and how our lives had changed based on the way we view life and death. And of course many of our family members have died since, but in every case - since my father had introduced all of them to this practice - the impact of people dying has left us with this amazing impression that "I'm going to live an amazing life the next go around!"

At the same time, our family - especially in the village where we were born - experienced quite a bit of paranormal activity. This left me with a lot of curiosity. So as I began to mature and grow up in this practice, I also began to read research.

I want to cite President Ikeda in his lecture on The Heritage of the Ultimate Law of Life. He refers to one of the big researchers on death and dying, Dr. Elisabeth Kubler-Ross. He mentions that Dr. Ross was on the psychiatric faculty of the University of Chicago. Although a Protestant, at that time she did not believe in life after death. But after 11 years of working with patients who were dying, she was forced to change her mind, and she now believes in the eternity of life.

She says: "At the first instant of death, the moment of physical separation is a good experience, like getting out of a prison. But the question is, what happens the next moment. What Christians call heaven or hell, the difference between good people and bad people, people who have led very enlightened lives and those who have not, comes afterwards, after separation. What Christians call hell is not as Christians describe it" She continues: "After they leave, they go through the walls...After they have passed over, comes what Christians would call hell. But there is no god who condemns you, but you are forced to review your own life. It's like watching a television screen, and your whole life is passed in front of you, not only deeds, but also thoughts. This is going through hell, because you see everything you have ever done and thought, and we may safely say then that some of the deceased go through heaven and others go through hell, depending on what they have accomplished and what they have been thinking throughout their life."

And later on I'll mention what some medical researchers, especially pediatricians, have done throughout the years.

PANEL DISCUSSION

Shinji Ishibashi

I think we have to understand that we can talk about theory, ultimate enlightenment, understanding of this Buddhism, but when it comes down to it, this means really developing confidence, really awakening to this Law to the point where it indeed becomes a part of our life. We don't scream when we go to bed - "Oh, no!; Oh,no!". We know we'll get up tomorrow. We develop confidence in the life cycle. I think this is the very reason Shakyamuni Buddha renounced his secular life and searched for the way of enlightenment. Until he was able to understand that, he was not able to relieve his suffering. So I'd like to propose that we talk about the subject of how we can live, in particular in the face of some loved one passing away. What is the correct attitude and how should we conduct ourselves.

Eric Hauber

Let me pick up where Shinji left off. I'm not really theoretical. What I like are stories, because stories make it possible for me to be in the story and think about what it means. When we were with President Ikeda in 1997, we were sitting around on the floor with him, and he just started talking. What he started talking about was life and death. He said, in one letter Nichiren Daishonin talks about death, and it's a horrible, ugly thing the way he describes death in this passage. He's describing the death of someone whose life is really in a suffering life condition at death - someone in a low life condition.

But President Ikeda said, that's not the death you will experience. Then what he said was: From the standpoint of the eternity of life, status or position are like a dream or an illusion.

When some people die, although they are unconscious, they die suffering. However, when we die - those of us who practice Nichiren Daishonin's Buddhism - we will stand on the summit of the highest mountain. The sunshine will pour over us and will illuminate the world for us. Then a beautiful, grand, white carriage will pick you up. Beautiful music will be playing, and inside that carriage it will not be hot the way it is inside a rocket, and then you will enjoy this flight into the universe as if you were floating. This white carriage will take you to a part of the universe to which you have always desired to go. In this universe, there are countless numbers of galaxies. You will be able to choose where you wish to be reborn, and when you are reborn on your favorite planet or your favorite galaxy, you will also choose the role that you will play again as an actor or actress in life. And once again, you will persevere in Buddhist practice, and in that next lifetime, you will again save many people, lead many people to happiness, and you will live a life of complete freedom and joy. This will be your life state. That is why, whether it be the status of a king or a prime minister, the Daishonin says that all of these things are an illusion. This is not my personal theory. I am only saying this in light of the Lotus Sutra and Nichiren Daishonin's writings. When you live out your life for the sake of world peace, and you are dedicating yourself and transcending life and death, you will be able to understand and feel what I am saying to you.

What President Ikeda described is the life condition, the feeling in our life, when we pass away.

He talked about Dick Causton - the late general director of the U.K. He said Dick Causton died an enlightened human being. He talked about what a noble person he was. Then he said, do you know what drives this process? - the part I just read about the white carriage and death? For me, that was the question I wanted answered. And he said, What determines what your life experiences when you die is the degree of compassion you carry in your heart when you breathe your last breath. He said, a person who has practiced sincerely as the Daishonin taught all their life amasses a tremendous life condition that is full of compassion because we take care of other people.

When you die in that way, that compassion is the force that carries your life throughout ku - the state of neither existence nor non-existence - it determines when your life is reborn, it determines how you are reborn, where you are reborn, and he said, a person who dies unenlightened, has the potential to have their life sucked into the bodies of little animals that are chased and devoured by cats. Or your life can reappear in grasses or trees, or as a human being. What determines this is the compassion you carry in your heart when you die. Because it's a natural order of the expression of life. Life will always manifest itself in such a way to be able to express the compassion which that life carries in its karmic condition. So, he said, the life form that is best able to express compassion is a human being. If you die with a life filled with compassion, absolutely you will be reborn very fast. You will be reborn together again with this practice, exactly as you yourself determine, in great circumstances.

And my thought was: How great is that! Then I thought - wait a second. That describes the life you all have now. Then I thought: We all must have lived magnificent lives in our last lifetime. Because all of us are reborn as human beings, we are reborn together with this practice in situations of fortune. And I thought: We are not starting over in the process of learning how to live and to die. We're continuing a process that deep in our life we already know. We may not be able to clearly define it, but our life knows. And, as President Ikeda says, as long as we continue to live our lives for the sake of world peace, for our own fortune and joy, as well as for others, we will absolutely find that white carriage and continue the life that we are developing today. And I thought: What an unbelievable way to think about our life! Because if you think about it, there's not a beginning or an end to your life. It's a continuation exactly of the moment, in the moment.

Teresa Hauber

First of all, from the Buddhist perspective, as we know, the four sufferings are birth, aging, sickness and death. And the whole purpose of Buddhism is: How can we create value? How can we become indestructibly happy, even though, as human beings, simply because we are born, we inevitably, without fail, are going to experience these four sufferings.

Did anyone see the movie Bicentennial Man? I thought it was great for this topic. Because it was a story of a very intelligent robot. They had put into his positronic brain the ability to think rationally and to come to conclusions very quickly. This robot had a thirst and a quest to constantly improve and be better, to start wearing clothes and skin, and as a result of his ability to input all of this scientific knowledge into his brain, he came up with all kinds of things that helped society.

The interesting thing was that the thing he strived for most was to be a human being, and he could not become a human being because he did not have the power to die. It wasn't until he could die that they could call him a human being. I thought that this was a very profound statement about life - that this whole aspect of dying or death is very intimately tied in with the very essence of life itself. And whether we have all this sophisticated knowledge about all the different consciousnesses, and that we can go to any galaxy and all that, is not the point. I think the point is, take any single moment and really ask ourselves: How can I change this moment? How can I create value in this moment? How can I become happier and more productive in this moment? Because life is only one moment after another, makes an hour, makes a week, makes a year. So constantly, not living in the distant past, or too far into the future, or wondering what I'm going to be when I'm 80 or 90, or where am I going the next lifetime, if we simply concentrate on this moment, and really determine to become indestructibly happy at this moment, to me these are very valuable tools that Buddhism has given my life. I find that sometimes I want everyone to chant Nam Myoho Renge Kyo. But sometimes people have very beautiful philosophies, and they love their philosophy. But no matter what a person embraces, they can always treasure each moment, they can always create value out of every moment. And if we can do this, as a society, I think we can really advance.

Margie Hall

I think it's in the last 10 years that I've wondered, what am I chanting when I'm chanting Nam Myoho Renge Kyo? In all my studies of this Buddhism, I've learned that Nam means basing my life upon, or having devotion to, Myoho - Myoho meaning Mystic Law. But what is that Mystic Law? I'm having faith in the fact that life is eternal; that life and death is the eternal cycle that we go through.

Over the last decade, I became very conscious of this. And then, over the last six years, I began to feel - not so much an intellectual thing - that I wanted to live every moment as though it were my last. And before I used to read about that all the time, and be really impressed with people who told me stories about that concept. But now, for the most part, I truly want to live that way. I'm very conscious of it. So it drives me very seriously.

I just want to cite a couple of authors. One is a Seattle pediatrician, Dr. Melvin Morse. He's done critical studies of childrens' near-death experiences, and we're really impressed with them because children are untainted; they are not conditioned by society. This is research he has done with children aged three and above, but especially the younger children.

One of his famous books is called "Closer to the Light", which has been reported in the pediatric journal of the American Medical Association. Some of the quotes in this book, which he got from these kids who spontaneously spoke to him throughout his practice as a pediatrician, were as follows:

> "I learned that everything in life is connected, and that if you hurt something, you hurt everything. I wasn't afraid to live again, because I knew that someday I would be with that light. I just wanted to be with that light...forget everything, I just wanted to get to that light. I heard a voice say, 'Go back, Bobby, you have a job to do.'"

Also this one other author George Anderson, one of his famous books is called "We don't die." I'm just citing these two authors because the information from their books, in my viewpoint, really supports what we believe in Nichiren Daishonin's Buddhism.

George Anderson gained the ability to hear voices and see visions from the other side after an illness at age six. Ever since 1973, he's been helping to counsel and comfort people. I just want to read this one little portion. When he was asked, Do those on the other side ever say how they would like to see us handle their passage?, he says: "They say unanimously that they wish we would try as best we can to realize that they have just moved on to the next stage of existence. They certainly don't want us to think that they don't understand our pain and grief, because they certainly do. They are often saddened to see how we suffer, and they do tell me of feeling frustrated because there's not very much they can do for us. They need us to realize that they are still alive, that they are here with us, that they care about us. They say they do benefit from prayer, so that is one thing we can do. They want us to be happy. They want us to know that we will all be together again."

QUESTIONS FROM THE AUDIENCE

Q. What's the Buddhist perspective on ghosts?

Theresa Hauber

I think, for me - and I don't want to speak as some kind of author ity on the subject - life is very mysterious, and I think we certainly don't know all of its dimensions. So I really like to listen to those kinds of things, and hear those kinds of things in terms of weighing and measuring them, and how can I use this to help people or myself gain value and become indestructibly happy. So if it works for me in this way, it is good.

The other thing, based on what Shinji had to say, is that we also have to realize that, from the perspective of this philosophy, Nichiren Daishonin's philosophy, we're talking about the ninth level of consciousness, that collective consciousness, that point of life when we are blended back into the universe. I think some of these experiences are still in the other levels of consciousness to help us gain understanding about life. That's just my feeling about that.

Shinji Ishibashi

I get calls from members telling me they can feel the person who has passed away, and the energy of the departed. That must be a sensitive person. I'm so dull at this kind of thing, if a ghost was tapping on my shoulder, I wouldn't even notice it. I think by us chanting Nam Myoho Renge Kyo for the happiness of all beings, and working toward the collective happiness of mankind, those energies that we are tapping in the ninth level of consciousness is definitely easing the pain of these people.

One thing I think we have to be careful of is not to mourn for these people. When someone dies, particularly the one we love, we have a very good excuse for feeling sorry and to cry and mourn for them. But if we allow ourself to do that, what will the deceased feel? They don't want to leave people behind crying. Again we have a justifiable reason for mourning, but by doing so, it's making it very difficult for their transition. Also their death becomes the cause for creating suffering. But even if we have every reason to moan and groan, if we really gather our courage and strength, and conduct ourselves in the brightest possible way, people will say "Wow, how did you get that kind of bright attitude? You're really touching me and inspiring me! Then the death of that person becomes the cause to create a person of great character. That becomes the cause of the deceased and they can take that with them. That's why, how we live this lifetime, how we continue to create value for ourself affects not only our own life, but the life of the deceased, literally to seven generations in the past and seven generations into the future. One single person who really challenges themselves to tap their fullest potential affects so many people in our realm of life. That's my understanding of Buddhism and how we live our life.

Eric Hauber

One thing President Ikeda has said is that when we practice we become aware of the profundity of life, and our own life. We become aware that there are many aspects of life that are far beyond our own understanding. So there are many teachings, there are many views. Some of them are incorrect, some are partially correct, some of them are very close. But the fundamental thing is that when we view them, bathed in the light of Buddhism, then we can begin to see clearly where the value is in each one. And I think it's an important thing for us who practice Buddhism to understand, as President Ikeda says, that we don't negate any of those teachings. What we do is illuminate them with the wisdom of Buddhism to find the value within them for us. To me, it's a lot more comfortable to approach it from that perspective.

Q.

I know of some people in the past few years who have committed suicide. What is the Buddhist perspective on people who take their own lives?

Eric Hauber

Many religious teachings are designed to make people feel good, regardless of what the situation is. Buddhism is a religion that says, let's see what the reality of life is. Let's look at it with all the good, the bad and the ugly, and then learn how to create value from seeing the reality.

Nichiren Daishonin is very clear and very specific that the greatest of all values in the universe is a human life. And therefore the greatest of negative causes is to take a life. There are two sides to this answer. Because in taking the life, whether it comes from suicide or whether it comes from murder, the taking of a life essentially denies the existence of the Law in that person's life. It's our slander of the Law in that person's life, and it's a serious cause.

When we have a loved one who has committed suicide, I think we are so fortunate that we chant, because no matter what cause that person made, there is always a cause that is greater than that cause, and that cause is to chant Nam Myoho Renge Kyo. If we have a loved one who has committed suicide, their life, wherever it is, is in a state in which they themselves cannot make a cause - one of the definitions of ku - and yet their ultimate fortune is that they have left behind yourself, me, loved ones, friends, fellow members who can chant for that life. And in the process of chanting for that life, we are able to polish that life, to increase the life condition of that life. We can hold that person within our own life. With our chanting, we polish their life and raise their life condition. So that at some point in the future, when they have the fortune to take on a physical form again, they will be able to move forward, to eventually become a Buddha.

So on the one hand it is absolutely a serious cause; but no matter how bad a cause it is, it is nowhere near as powerful a cause you make to chant Nam Myoho Renge Kyo for their life. So it is not an end, and there is hope. In Buddhism, there is always hope.

Question:

Since I have started practicing, I have not been afraid of death, and I've had some glorious experiences with family members in this area. My personal karma has been to be alone - and my life tendency and karma is - alone. And my question is, how do you turn that karma into value. I know part of my answer is to have been a part of this organization. My being a teacher...everything has to do with being alone - no family. My pain is that this is my karma at this point in my life. And I'm sure there are other people in the room who have experiences similar to this.

Shinji Ishibashi

Imagine if you had not practiced, where you could have been. We tend to focus on what we don't have, and don't take time to really realize what we have. I think you have accomplished so much. For you to come to this point to be able to share that very pain in front of people itself requires tremendous courage. I think you are touching many peoples' hearts right now as you speak.

President Ikeda says: "A truly great person is a friend to those in suffering, pain and misery. Such a person can be called a leader of the new century."

I think we tend to judge ourself in a relative scale with others, always looking around and seeing where we are at with the rest of the people. If we are doing better than others, we think we are doing good. That means we have to outdo others all the time. Now we can become very good at this. 99.9% of the time, we can outdo people. That means 999 out of 1000, we can outdo people. If that's the basis from which we feel our sense of security, that one person out of a thousand can make us feel back to zero again.

So President Ikeda continously encourages us not to compare ourselves to others. "Do not compare yourself to others," he writes. "Be true to who you are, and continue to learn with all your might, even if you are ridiculed. Even if you suffer disappointment and setbacks, continue to advance and do not be defeated. If you have such a strong determination in your heart, you are already halfway to the victory. It's not important how you compare to others, but how you compare to who you were yesterday. If you see that you have advanced even one step, then you have achieved a victory."

Don't you think you have achieved lots of victories? Don't you think so?

Question:

What do you do when you're eight years old, and you find out you are going to die?

Margie Hall

Just based on my readings of these books by pediatricians, depending on the views of the support group around the child - and let's say the humanism of the doctors and nurses - the eight year old who has that really great support group is going to have a really great attitude about the fact that they are just going to go into another phase. But children who did not have such a great experience, I think, are not dissimilar to the experiences of adults who have such support groups or non-supportive groups. So I think for those of us who practice this Buddhism, that we can be the greatest support group. As we're entering the 21st century, more and more people are becoming aware that there is a great need for humanistic behavior. Because there are just too many killings going on, especially by the youth. I think it's waking people up to the fact that we really have to do something and it makes me really think about President Ikeda and his speeches and lectures and guidance, the fact that we can chant

Nam Myoho Renge Kyo every day, and revolutionize our lives in the very fundamental depths.

I thought this one great example was given to me about death, that when you die, it's like the waves of the ocean as they come up and then go back into the ocean. You don't know which life you are going to be next, but it's like that, you meld back into the ocean of the universe. So what is remaining in the core of that passing life? What is at the core? That's what I think about, and I'm really appreciative when I chant every morning and evening, that at the core of my life I have this philosophy and this view of life, that I can merge back into the greater universe and really contribute to the next life that I'm going to be a part of.

Question:

My mother at this moment is in intensive care in the hospital, dying. We have been very close, and I've never experienced such pain. I love this woman. I'm chanting for her, but at the same time, my life is so filled with pain. My question is, when I'm in such a life condition and suffering, how effective is my chanting? How much is my chanting automatically affecting things, even though I'm in so much pain?

Teresa Hauber

Regardless of what you do, crying, sobbing, pulling your hair out, jumping with joy, kissing, your chanting is ultimately reaching her life at a very profound and very deep level. Remember chanting Nam Myoho Renge Kyo is not a mind game. It isn't that if you think the perfect thought while you are chanting, you get a better result. Chanting is chanting. It's like breathing the air. It's like drinking the milk or eating the food. I can have a delicious piece of cherry pie and the way it's going to break down biochemically in the body is the same, regardless of what I'm thinking, even if I was thinking some other thought that was saying that this is not going to break down in my body. It's going to break down in my body because I took it in. It's the same with Nam Myoho Renge Kyo, it's exactly that fundamental. In one of Nichiren Daishonin's letters, On Prayer, it says "One might ask why the results of these vows should be so long in appearing, and yet, though one might point an arrow at the earth and miss it, though one might bind up the sky, though the tides might cease to ebb and flow, and the sun rise in the west, it could never come about that the prayers of the practitioner of the Lotus Sutra would go unanswered."

So whatever your prayer is, without fail, it absolutely will be answered, even if we say "I'm going to chant, but it's not going to be answered." It will be answered. We're human beings and we're going to feel these various things. It's okay to feel them. It's not going to affect the power of Nam Myoho Renge Kyo.

Question:

I wanted to direct this question to Margie. You talked about near death experiences, and people having memories of them, and I've heard also that when these experiences have been recorded, there's a similarity between them, that people go through a dark tunnel and then they see a light. My question is, these experiences seem kind of hit and miss, because I have known people who died and did come back and did not have a conscious memory of that, and I wonder why that is so.

Margie Hall

I did not bring the book with me, but I know President Ikeda has referred to the multi-dimensional aspect of life, and I think Eric Hauber touched on this earlier, that for those of us who practice this Buddhism, we become more conscious and sensitive and aware of the kinds of causes we make, due to the multi-dimensionality of life. It depends on the person, whether that individual is going to have such experiences, and it's very subjective.

In response to the question before, I had one of those instances happen when I perceived a ghost. This was in Hawaii, and I flipped out, because it happened over a period of a week. I knew I was not hallucinating. At that time, I received guidance from a leader in the Soka Gakkai. He told me that, because I was in such a hellish life condition during that period of time, I pulled out something from the universe which was manifested in the house where I was living. Then later on, I learned that the previous owner of the house had died a pretty miserable death. I learned the name of this person because the guidance I was given was that obviously the energy that was left behind somehow connected with the hellish condition that I was going through. So this person giving me guidance gave me this very amazing perspective: "Please chant for this entity. Because he is in an inactive state, he cannot do anything for himself. Somehow you were able to manifest this in your own hell, but now you can change it into enlightenment, not only for yourself, but for this other person."

So I feel that it really depends on the person, and who am I to judge what experience that person might have. But I know in talking to many, many members over the years I do not discount anything that people tell me. The experiences are varied and sometimes far-out, but my attitude is, I believe everything that person has to say to me, and then I try to come from the viewpoint of Nichiren Daishonin's Buddhism to really alleviate their suffering, as this person did for me.

Question:

What about people who are strong practicing members who have suffered an untimely death, such as plane crashes, car crashes, murders. Could you give us a perspective on this?

Eric Hauber

I would like to share a story that someone told me about being at dinner with President Ikeda four or five years ago, and they were having a conversation about someone who had died in a fire. And what President Ikeda said is, does that mean then if someone dies this kind of death, they did not die an enlightened person? He said absolutely not. That's one way to die. He said the way in which people die is also the way in which they change karma. The way to know whether or not that person died an enlightened human being is not to look so much at the way they died, but to look at the loved ones they leave behind. If you look at the families and loved ones of those people, the dead person's fortune will manifest itself in the condition of that family. Now it's certainly a charge to those of us in that family who are left behind. To me it was a great answer because it was not a simple answer, and it implied the profundity of life, and that easy and quick answers are not necessarily the true and only answer.

Shinji Ishibashi

We are still operating on the assumption that dying is bad. President Ikeda has often said that the quality of life is not measured by how long we live but by how meaningful a life we live. I think we continue to struggle with this subject. But we need to challenge ourselves to really experience the joy of life by living it fully each moment and to reach the life condition - not so much the theoretical understanding - where our life reaches the conviction and confidence that indeed in living our life to the fullest, the age at which we die is not the really significant point about life. When we come to the end of life, we all have to go. That's the immutable karma. We might extend our life a few months or years by still having a mission to fulfill and praying earnestly that we might be able to do that, but still death is inevitable. So, again, it's not that dying is bad. Rather, how meaningful a life we live is ultimately our challenge.

Eric Hauber

I want to share another of President Ikeda's stories that directly relates to this. Vice President Matsushima, who is the editor in chief of the Seikyo Shimbun, was here in 1993 when President Ikeda was here. We had the opportunity to talk to him. He had used the term "true dialogue" and we asked him what was "true dialogue", as opposed to other kinds of dialogue. And he told us this story.

He said he was standing two years before that on a street corner in Tokyo in 1991 with President Ikeda, waiting for something, and he said President Ikeda said that while they were waiting, he thought he would go across the street and take a walk. Well, across the street was a cemetery. And the people with him sort of questioned him, wondering why he would want to do that. And he said, you don't understand. That's a most joyful place. He said when I go across the street and I walk there, I carry on a heart to heart dialogue with all the people who are there. And they say, "Here comes Daisaku Ikeda, let's have a dialogue!" And he said, I have a dialogue with each one of them. But the interesting thing was, he talked about them in the present tense, not the past tense. And then Mr. Matsushima said that clearly they had a puzzled look on their faces, because President Ikeda said: True dialogue is not words. True dialogue is life to life, heart to heart, and you can carry on true dialogue with anyone - past, present or future, at any time. With Nam Myoho Renge Kyo, the Mystic Law, there's no time or space.

We all want to talk about this, because we all have loved ones who have passed away. My father died in 1984, so I had the same question you had. And what President Ikeda said was, we think because someone has died, we feel like they have ceased to exist. But in actuality that life exists as real now as it was back before they passed away. The difference is we don't see them in a physical form. He said, you can carry on a dialogue with one of your deceased loved ones. You can chant Nam Myoho Renge Kyo. You can visualize them. And at that moment, as your life is fused with the Mystic Law, you hold that person in your life. You can carry on a dialogue with them. You can polish their life. You can put into their life what you want them to get. And it's the same thing with people who are alive.

Then we said, we understand that, but what about the future? And what he said was, future is the same as past. Past is defined because these are people we no longer see. Future is exactly the same, it's just that these are people whom we have not seen yet. So he said, you can carry on a conversation with a person in the future.

This one young woman who was there started to cry. And he said to her, if you have a determination that someday you want to be a mother and have a child, why can't you begin a dialogue with your unborn child now.

And I thought, how magnificent it must be, to be a mother or father like that. And chanting abut that experience, and particularly my father, taught me a lot about death. Because if you think about this group over here as past, simply we don't see them anymore; this group is present, some of those we don't see anymore either; and over here is the future - people we have yet to see. But if you take them all as one big group, it's all life. It all exists. And we cycle through times of being seen, not being seen, being physical, not being physical; but it's all one magnificent life. It's Myoho Renge Kyo.

Q. About breaking the cycle of birth and death. I have been reading about this subject, and I would like your perspectives.

Theresa Hauber

When we talk about breaking the cycle of birth and death, it doesn't mean that physiologically our material aspect doesn't go through the process. Even the earth we are on today is going through the whole process of formation and decline. So anything material, anything that has a physical aspect, is going to decline. I think when they talk about breaking the cycle of birth and death, I think it refers to your understanding of the essence of life itself. And the way you create value or make decisions is based more on the eternal factor. President Ikeda said in the book "Life: An Enigma; A Precious Jewel", something to the effect that we need to live our life in the reality of every day, but never losing sight of the ninth consciousness. The ninth consciousness is that Nam Myoho Renge Kyo consciousness, the eternity of life. So when you think about that then, maybe some of the ways you prioritize your daily actions will be different. Or the way we interact with someone will be different. Maybe when we speak to someone, it might be more heart-to-heart, rather than just trying to get the job done.

So in that respect, you cannot physically never not die. Even a house or a plant or a tree, or something that's lived 10,000 years, eventually is going to die. So is the earth. But the point is that life itself can never be eliminated. It has really no beginning and no end and that's the eternity of life. And as soon as we become aware of that, we begin to understand our own Buddhahood. So when they talk about breaking the cycle, it means your own awareness of the essence of life itself.

Shinji Ishibashi

By breaking, do you mean being no longer subject to the cycle of birth and death?

(Response: Yes).

The Nirvana Sutra talks specifically about this. This is the expedient means. By supposedly going through this process of enlightenment, they interpret enlightenment as being above the cycle. So they created this term nirvana as an expedient way of explaining this, but it's not totally correct. No one can break the cycle.

Nirvana simply means nothing, zero, does not exist anymore. They thought the ultimate form of enlightenment is to become nothingness, to become the universe itself. Again that was the expedient means. Life never disappears, it is a continuous ebb and flow, continuing on. That's what life is. How we live the living phase is what determines our life. We always have this choice to make every single moment. We have no control of the past, we have no control of the future; but this very moment, how we determine to live literally changes the past as well as the future. That is the aspect of complete freedom and control that we possess within us.

And by tapping that purity of life, we become a person free of self-interest. The only interest that we possess is to exist for the sake of the happiness of others. That's the challenge. I said challenge, because nobody's there. The concept of heaven described in Christianity for example, is a place where you have no pain; wonderful music playing all the time, wonderful joy all the time. But of course you cut off the music sometimes, because you don't want music all the time. What makes good music is lousy music. A short person makes another person tall. So if we eliminate all those elements from our life, and call it heaven, it never exists. We appreciate our health when we are hospitalized. That's the essence of the universe. All of these things are contained in our life. And, again, to live our life to the fullest, is ultimately our goal. So I'm sorry to disappoint you, there's no way we can break the chain.

AN EXPERIENCE
BY LING LING CHEN

My name is Ling. I was born in Taiwan. I grew up in a Chinese Buddhist background. I came to the United States and was married on the east coast in 1979. The marriage did not work out, though, and I came to California with my two children in 1985.

I was introduced to the SGI and Nichiren Daishonin's Buddhism in 1987 by a friend who lived in San Diego. Because of the distance between us, she introduced me to a woman named Nancy living in Los Angeles. Nancy was very persistent in helping me to practice. She knew by practicing this Buddhism, I could change my life condition and become truly happy.

For the first few months, I did not have much faith that the practice really worked, and as a result I did not chant. Nancy kept telling me to ask for something, just try it.

I was a single mother, raising two children alone. I was working three jobs, the main one as a bartender at a bowling alley. The jobs were all at different places, and it was a big distance between jobs. Sometimes I would fall asleep on my job.

Finding a trustworthy, responsible baby sitter was a big challenge to me. Nancy told me that by chanting I would get what I needed to be happy, so I began chanting for a baby sitter. A week later, I was late for work one day because I had no baby sitter, and a girl who lived downstairs, who I had seen before but who I did not know, just came up to me and asked: "Do you want a babysitter?

It turned out that her grandmother, an older Vietnamese lady with whom she lived, was looking for a job as a babysitter. I hired the grandmother, and she became like a mother to my own children, and eventually she began practicing also.

That day I chanted with overwhelming appreciation. My faith immediately became so strong, from just this one little thing.

That same day, because I was late for work from looking for a babysitter, I was fired from my main job. But to me it was not a negative thing, because I thought right away, okay I'm going to chant for another job. I wrote down exactly the money I wanted. I wanted one job that would pay as much as my three other jobs. I also wanted the job to be within fifteen minutes of where I lived. One week later I got exactly that job. It paid more than my three previous jobs, and I timed the distance on the way home, and it was less than fifteen minutes.

As a result of this experience, I introduced three of my friends to this Buddhism.

My job was so good. I was making a lot of money, and I was able to save up enough money to start my own business up north in Fairfield, California in 1989. I started a gift shop business. I visited all the military bases and contracted with them to set up concessions at the bases. I became so busy with my new business, that my practice suffered. Human nature is such that when everything is going great you forget how you got there. You lose appreciation. I became more involved in my personal life and started practicing less and less. My business gradually declined, and within a year's time I lost everything. I had to close my business. I moved back to Los Angeles in 1990. I had stopped practicing.

For the next eight or nine years, I had no religion, no belief. Still, all this time, every now and then I chanted. Inside my heart, I still had Nam Myoho Renge Kyo. It never went away.

Then in 1999, my life took an enormous turn. I was at home, and my son was in his room playing loud music. Suddenly, there was a very loud sound. I went into his room and found my son. He had shot himself in the head with a gun, playing Russian roulette.

When I found my son's body, I immediately began chanting. On the arrival of the paramedics, I was still chanting. I chanted all the way to the hospital.

After my son's death, I experienced such a deep unhappiness. Many people tried to help me. A friend of mine, also from Taiwan, seeing me suffer so much, began aggressively encouraging me to visit a Buddhist Temple - the same Chinese Buddhist sect I was brought up in. I participated in the ceremonies, but somehow I did not feel peace. I felt out of place and I had this deep consuming pain that would not go away. I did not get any comfort. My life was in this dark hole, and was going in deeper and deeper. I wanted someone to just bury me. I even wished that something more tragic would happen to take away the pain. I felt like dying, but I couldn't kill myself because I could not take my family, my daughter, my mother, my brother through the same pain I was feeling.

An American friend took me to a Christian church. I talked to the pastor who told me "He's with God. God made him an angel."

It was all about God. I thought, if God is so powerful, that he could create this whole world, why did he need my son? I went to a regular church service. The pastor was talking of God. I was crying all the time. I really wanted to know why God took my son. I stood up and said: “If you’re the messenger of God, please give me back my son. Why did you make him an angel?” People wanted me to be quiet.

I also went to group therapy. Everyone had lost a loved one. I did not like that either. Everyone was so concerned with their own pain, searching for answers also.

There were no answers. There was no hope.

My Chinese friend could see that I was not getting better, so she took me back to a girl she knew in the SGI. This girl, in turn, called Nancy, whom I had not seen in several years, and mystically Nancy reappeared again in my life. Nancy immediately came over. She arranged for me to talk to a leader in the SGI. I told this man, I want my son back. He told me if I chanted Nam Myoho Renge Kyo, I would get my son back. I would see my son again. He gave me the answer I was looking for. He gave me what I wanted. I felt hope, and I began chanting Nam Myoho Renge Kyo again.

After this, I began to see a little flicker of light in that deep hole I was in. Little by little, every day, in the car, every chance I got, I chanted. Members would come to my house to chant with me and to encourage me morning and evening. When I chanted, I did not ask for anything for myself, not for my pain to go away or anything for myself. I chanted sincerely to see my son again. I chanted because I wanted my son back. I was still in much pain and going through deep depression. My hope, focus and faith was that no matter what, I would see my son again.

Little by little, through my chanting, and talking with others and studying this Buddhism, my understanding of this practice and my life deepened immeasurably. I came to understand my life and also my son's life, and how we are connected. I came to see that my son had had the karma to die young in the manner he did, but that at the same time his mission was to give me this Buddhism, so that I can change my karma and at the same time change his karma, so that in this life or next lifetime or whenever we meet again, we won't have a short 15 or 16 year relationship, we can have a long wonderful relationship. We are making progress to change both our karma by my practice. I am working to change my own life, to become happy, so that I can lead my son to happiness.

Through chanting for my son to come back, I faced my pain and sadness. I determined that I will live with hope. In a way, he gave his life to save me. That was his mission, to help me to understand my life, and the eternity of life. So when I look at it this way, then I cannot be sad anymore. My job is to change my karma and to become happy. For some reason, by chanting my pain became a different kind of pain and a different kind of suffering. Somehow Nam Myoho Renge Kyo gave me the strength to face my life. Without this tragedy, I probably would never have practiced and come to understand my life and my son's life and to deepen my faith and understanding. Through chanting, this tragedy became the deepest benefit imaginable.

One day - I really remember this - I was with a group of people, and I found myself smiling. I could hardly realize it was me. I had to stop and think - is this me laughing? Because I truly thought I would not laugh again. At that moment, my faith deepened. I realized that all this time I was changing. The pain was still there, but I was becoming happy again.

Now I laugh all the time. I'm very happy. Life is wonderful. I really appreciate life and try to do the best I can each day, to treat people kindly and help them.

Life is good! I cannot believe sometimes that I say this. Just to be able to enjoy. When I had my first benefit, the baby sitter, I was happy. But now it's a different stage of my life, my life condition is different. I chant a lot. I don't ask for benefit. When I chant, I connect with Nam Myoho Renge Kyo, nothing else. I believe Nam Myoho Renge Kyo will lead me to where I have to be in life, and that's happiness.

I have a sales job on commission. When I started out, I had 80 accounts. Now I have 30 accounts, but in the last year I have doubled the money I am making.

I'm discovering talents I never knew I had. I've taken up painting and to my surprise people tell me I'm quite good, and it also gives me much joy. My life has changed drastically due to this whole experience. The loss of my son's life gave me the desire to live my life to the fullest. I will never abandon my faith again.

Quoting President Ikeda: "Buddhism was expounded precisely so as to enable the discriminated and oppressed, those who have experienced the bitterest sufferings, to attain supreme happiness. This is the power of Buddhism, and the true wisdom of the Lotus Sutra."

BIBLIOGRAPHY AND RECOMMENDED READING

Capra, Fritjof; The Tao of Physics. Boston, Shambhala Publications, Inc., 2000.

Hochswender, Martin, Morino; The Buddha in Your Mirror. Santa Monica, Middleway Press, 2001.

Ikeda, Daisaku; Life: An Enigma, a Precious Jewel. New York, Kodansha International, Ltd., 1982.

Ikeda, Daisaku; The Human Revolution. Los Angeles, The World Tribune Press, 1988.

Ikeda, Daisaku & Wilson, Bryan, Human Values in a Changing World. New Jersey, Lyle Stuart Inc., 1987.

Ikeda, Daisaku; The Wisdom of the Lotus Sutra. Santa Monica, World Tribune Press, 2000.

Ikeda, Daisaku; For the Sake of Peace. Santa Monica, Middleway Press, 2000.

Ikeda, Daisaku; The Way of Youth. Santa Monica, Middleway Press, 2001.

Ikeda, Daisaku; Soka Education. Santa Monica, Middleway Press, 2001.

Ikeda, Daisaku; The Living Buddha. Connecticut, Weatherhill, Inc., 1976.

Ikeda, Daisaku; Unlocking the Mysteries of Birth and Death: Buddhism in the Contemporary World. London, MacDonald & Co. Ltd., 1988.

Jung, Carl; Memories, Dreams, Reflections. New York, Vintage Books, 1989.

Kubler-Ross, Elisabeth; On Death and Dying. New York, Touchstone, 1997.

Kubler-Ross, Elisabeth; On Life after Death. Berkeley, Celestial Arts, 1991.

Moody, Raymond A. Jr.; The Light Beyond. New York, Bantam Books, 1988.

Muir, John; John Muir: Nature Writings. New York, The Library of America, 1997.

Nichiren Daishonin; The Writings of Nichiren Daishonin. Tokyo, Soka Gakkai, 1999.

Ring, Kenneth; Life at Death. New York, William Morrow and Company, Inc., 1982.

Sugrue, Thomas; There is a River. Edgar Cayce Foundation, Virginia Beach, Virginia, 1989.

Tolstoy, Leo; The Death of Ivan Ilyich.

Watson, Burton, translator; The Lotus Sutra. New York, Columbia University Press, 1993.

Wheeler, John Archibald; From The Physicist's Conception of Nature, edited by Jagdish Mehra. Boston, D. Reidel Publishing Company, 1973.

INDEX

INDEX

ABOUT THE AUTHOR AND PANEL PARTICIPANTS

Author James Hilgendorf is co-producer, with his brother John, of the acclaimed travel and culture video series, The Tribute Series.

Panel Discussion Participants:

Margie Hall is a former editor of Living Buddhism, a monthly journal of the SGI-USA, and is currently in charge of the organization department of the SGI-USA.

Eric Hauber is Vice President for Enrollment Services and Long Range Planning at Soka University of America, Aliso Viejo, California.

Theresa Hauber is a Clinical Supervisor with Saddleback Coordinated Homecare.

Shinji Ishibashi is President of Summit Architects, Santa Monica.

Both the author and panel members live in the Los Angeles area, and all are long-time practicing members of the SGI, or Soka Gakkai International, a Buddhist lay organization active in 187 countries throughout the world.

THE TRIBUTE SERIES

The Tribute Series is the publisher of this book, as well as the producer of a unique series of video films - The Tribute Series - combining travel, history, interviews with local people, and beautiful photography, whose purpose is to build bridges of friendship and understanding between different cultures and peoples of the world.

The Seattle Times says:

> "No one is better at revealing the heart of a place than brothers Jim and John Hilgendorf."

Tribute Series films are in homes, schools, and libraries throughout the United States, and have aired on PBS television in the United States, as well as being broadcast on international television.

Current titles include films on India, Tuscany & Umbria, Mexico, California, New England, St.Petersburg, Russia, Indiana, Ireland, Cape Town, South Africa, and Munich & Southern Germany.

More information is available online at www.tributeseries.com, or by telephone at (800) 898-9441. The Tribute Series, P.O.Box 195, Vida, Oregon, 97488.

SGI-USA DIRECTORY

For those wishing to know more about the lay Buddhist organization of the SGI, or Soka Gakkai International, or who are interested in attending a discussion meeting in your area, the following telephone contacts throughout the United States are listed.

NATIONAL SGI-USA HEADQUARTERS

SGI PLAZA 606 Wilshire Blvd. Santa Monica, CA 90401	(310) 260-8900

CULTURE CENTERS AND COMMUNITY CENTERS

ALASKA	Alaska Community Center 2702 Gambell St., Suite 200 Anchorage, AK 99503	(907)274-8889
ARIZONA	Phoenix Community Center 1930 E. Myrtle Avenue Phoenix, AZ 85020	(602)263-7900
	Tucson Community Center 2540 E. 22nd Street Tucson, AZ 85713	(520)323-8184

CALIFORNIA	East Bay Community Center 9943 San Pablo Avenue El Cerrito, CA 94530	(510)527-4402
	E. Los Angeles Community Center 747 Del Valle Avenue La Puente, CA 91744	(626)968-1788
	Fresno Activity Center 4747 N. First Street, Suite 120 Fresno, CA 93726	(559)221-4653
	Los Angeles Friendship Center 5899 Venice Blvd. Los Angeles, CA 90019	(323)965-0025
	North San Diego Community Ctr. 800 Los Vallecitos Blvd., Ste. C&D San Marcos, CA 92069	(760)591-9738
	Riverside Community Center 1120 Palmyrita Avenue Riverside, CA 92507	(909)683-8760
	Sacramento Community Center 2230 Arden Way, Suite D Sacramento, CA 95825	(916)564-4700
	San Diego Community Center 4828 Ronson Court San Diego, CA 92111	(858)514-3870
	San Fernando Community Center 14840 Nordhoff Street Panorama City, CA 91402	(818)830-1336
	San Francisco Culture Center 2450 17th Street San Francisco, CA 94110	(415)255-6007

	Santa Ana Community Center 1500 Brookhollow Drive Santa Ana, CA 92705	(714)444-9580
	Santa Barbara Community Center 5324-A Ekwill Street Goleta, CA 93117	(805)681-7494
	Santa Monica Community Center 2601 Pico Blvd. Santa Monica, CA 90405	(310)829-1005
	Santa Rosa Community Center 2455 Bennett Valley Road,Ste.A100 Santa Rosa, CA. 95404	(707)546-7777
	Silicon Valley Community Center 1875 De La Cruz Avenue Santa Clara, CA 95050	(408)727-2604
	South Bay Community Center 20300 S. Vermont Ave., #105 Torrance, CA 90502	(310)856-4280
	Valley Community Center 14836 Nordhoff Street Panorama City, CA 91402	(818)830-1344
COLORADO	Colorado Springs Community Ctr. 703 No. Arrawanna Street Colorado Springs, CO 80909	(719)635-8968
	Denver Culture Center 1450 N. Speer Blvd. Denver, CO 80204	(303)893-0430
CONNECTICUT	Connecticut Activity Center 518 Boston Post Road Orange, CT 06477	(203)799-0512

FLORIDA	Florida Nature & Culture Center 20000 SW 36th Street Ft. Lauderdale, FL 33332	(954)349-5000
	Miami Community Center 20000 SW 36th Street Ft. Lauderdale, FL 33332	(954)349-5200
	Orlando Community Center 452-1 North Semoran Blvd. Orlando, FL 32807	(407)482-3939
	Pensacola Activity Center 430 Bryn Athyn Blvd., Unit 1 Mary Esther, FL 32569	(850)986-2454
	Tampa Activity Center 2047 5th Avenue North St. Petersburg, FL 33713	(727)328-3626
GEORGIA	Atlanta Community Center 5831 Riverdale Road College Park, GA 30349	(770)996-5178
GUAM	Guam Community Center P.O. Box 7117 Tamuning, Guam 96931	011671-646-4737
HAWAII	Hawaii Culture Center 2729 Pali Highway Honolulu, HI 96817	(808)595-6324
	Hilo Community Center 695 Makalika Street Hilo, HI 96720	(808)959-0701
	Kauai Activity Center 4211 Rice Street, Suite M5 Lihue, HI 96766	(808)632-2247

	Makaha Community Center 84-610 Lahaina Street Waianae, HI 96792	(808)695-8911
	Maui Community Center 810 Kolu Street Wailuku, Maui HI 96793	(808)244-5614
	Pupukea Community Center 59-318 Alapio Road Haleiwa, HI 96712	(808)638-7220
ILLINOIS	Chicago Culture Center 1455 South Wabash Avenue Chicago, IL 60605	(312)913-1211
INDIANA	Indiana Community Center 2126 N. Mitthoeffer Road Indianapolis, IN 46229	(317)898-1497
KENTUCKY	Kentucky Community Center 1930 Bardstown Road Louisville, KY 40205	(502)454-6100
LOUISIANA	New Orleans Community Center 2926 Canal Street New Orleans, LA 70119	(504)827-9965
MARYLAND	Baltimore Community Center 1583 Sulphur Spring Rd., Suite 118 Arbutus, MD 21227	(410)536-5766
	Washington, D.C. Community Ctr. 4603 Eastern Avenue Mt. Rainier, MD 20712	(301)779-3255
MASSA- CHUSETTS	New England Culture Center 545 Main Street Waltham, MA 02452	(781)642-8887

MINNESOTA	Minnesota Community Center 1381 Eustis Street St. Paul, MN 55108	(651)645-3133
MISSOURI	Kansas City Community Center 1804 Broadway Street Kansas City, MO 64108	(816)474-7973
	St. Louis Community Center 9126 St. Charles Rock Road St. Louis, MO 63114	(314)427-0585
NEBRASKA	Omaha Community Center 1021 North 46th Street Omaha, NE 68132	(402)558-6148
NEVADA	Las Vegas Community Center 1201 So. Jones Blvd., Suite A Las Vegas, NV 89102	(702)258-6489
NEW JERSEY	New Jersey Community Center 60 Franklin Street East Orange, NJ 07017	(973)395-1180
	South Jersey Community Center Route 168 Turnersville, NJ 08012	(856)227-9110
NEW MEXICO	Albuquerque Community Center 1911 Sunshine Terrace SE Albuquerque, NM 87106	(505)843-6031
NEW YORK	New York Culture Center 7 East 15th Street New York, NY 10003	(212)727-7715
	Buffalo Community Center 531 Virginia Street Buffalo, NY 14202	(716)856-2623

State	Center	Phone
	Hudson Valley Activity Center 75 South Broadway White Plains, NY 10601	(914)287-2063
N. CAROLINA	North Carolina Community Center 6307 Chapel Hill Road Raleigh, NC 27607	(919)859-0112
	East Carolina Activity Center 4355-A Gum Branch Road Jacksonville, NC 28546	(910)937-7652
OHIO	Cleveland Community Center 13111 Crossburn Avenue Cleveland, OH 44135	(216)265-0974
	Columbus Community Center 1197 Noe-Bixby Road Columbus, OH 43213	(614)751-8990
OKLAHOMA	Oklahoma Community Center 3800 N. Cromwell Avenue Oklahoma City, OK 73112	(405)947-1101
OREGON	Eugene Community Center 2160 W. 11th Avenue, Suite B Eugene, OR 97402	(541)345-8486
	Portland Community Center 1805 S. E. Ankeny Street Portland, OR 97214	(503)230-1038
PENNSYL-VANIA	Philadelphia Community Center 2000 Hamilton Street, Suite 210 Philadelphia, PA 19130	(215)569-2144
	Pittsburgh Community Center 2121 Noblestown Road, Suite 310 Pittsburgh, PA 15205	(412)919-0200

PUERTO RICO	Puerto Rico Community Center Centro Comunal de Laguna Gardens Carreterra Marginal de Condominios Laguna Gardens Isla Verde, Puerto Rico 00913	(787)791-3118
S. CAROLINA	South Carolina Community Center 1911 Hampton Street Columbia, SC 29201	(803)252-7838
TENNESSEE	Memphis Community Center 840 S. Highland Street Memphis, TN 38111	(901)452-6153
TEXAS	Austin Activity Center 5555 N. Lamar Blvd., Suite #C-109 Austin, TX 78751	(512)323-9191
	Dallas Culture Center 2733 Oak Lawn Avenue Dallas, TX 75219	(214)559-4115
	El Paso Commnity Center 2901 No. Campbell Street El Paso, TX 79902	(915)534-7022
	Houston Community Center 3465 W. Alabama, Suite B Houston, TX 77027	(713)622-6181
	San Antonio Community Center 8030 Cross Creek San Antonio, TX 78218	(210)653-7755
TRINIDAD	Trinidad Community Center 121 Henry Street Port of St. James Trinidad, West Indies	(868)625-3121

UTAH	Salt Lake Community Center 537 East 300 South Salt Lake City, UT 84102	(801)538-0822
VIRGINIA	Northern Virginia Activity Center 7400 Fullerton Road, Suite 107 Springfield, VA 22153	(703)451-0441
	Southeast Virginia Activity Center 5476 Virginia Beach Blvd, Ste. 101 Virginia Beach, VA 23462	(757)490-3366
WASHINGTON	Seattle Culture Center 3438 South 148th Street Seattle, WA 98168	(206)244-0268
	Spokane Community Center 8019 W. Sunset Hwy. Spokane, WA 99224	(509)747-0990
	Tacoma Community Center 8815 S. Tacoma Way, Suite 112 Tacoma, WA 98499	(253)582-8520

Printed in the United States
16593LVS00001B/274-276